WITHDRAWN

WOMEN RACERS

Inside Stories in the Fast Lane

WITHDRAWN

Glenda J. Fordham

OVER
TIME
BOOKS

© 2007 by OverTime Books

First printed in 2007 10 9 8 7 6 5 4 3 2 1

Printed in Canada

All rights reserved. No part of this work covered by the copy-rights hereon may be reproduced or used in any form or by any means—graphic, electronic or mechanical—without the prior written permission of the publisher, except for reviewers, who may quote brief passages. Any request for photocopying, recording, taping or storage on information retrieval systems of any part of this work shall be directed in writing to the publisher.

The Publisher: OverTime Books is an imprint of Éditions de la Montagne Verte

Library and Archives Canada Cataloguing in Publication

Fordham, Glenda J., 1953–

    Women racers / Glenda Fordham.

Includes bibliographical references.

ISBN-10: 1-897277-15-6

ISBN-13: 978-1-897277-15-7

    1. Women automobile racing drivers—Biography. I. Title.

GV1032.A1F675 2007   796.72092'2   C2007-906147-8

Project Director: J. Alexander Poulton

Editor: Jordan Allan

Cover: Courtesy of Getty Images Sport/Jamie Squire, photographer

PC: 5

Dedication

This book is dedicated to Ashley Taws, whose bright pink "Barbie at Wal-Mart" Formula 1600 BMW inspires little girls across the country to dream big; and to the brilliant Katherine Legge, who proves in every race she runs that women can do anything they set their minds to; and to Glenna Chestnutt, whose own dream to compete in the grueling Dakar Rally in 2009 is becoming a reality. You go, girls!

Contents

WOMEN OF THE NEW MILLENIUM

Acknowledgments

I would like to express my gratitude to all those friends and associates who fueled me with cups of coffee and lots of encouragement over the long days and nights researching and writing this book. Special thanks go out to Rob Huntley, publisher of BrakeTest.net, and to Laura Lang of Inside Track magazine.

My thanks also to all the drivers and race teams who kindly allowed me entry into their world, and to the wonderful crew at the Steelback Grand Prix of Toronto, especially Andrea Hynes, who helped make this all possible.

A History of Women in Motorsports: An Introduction or Eve takes the Wheel

Many Christmases ago, I remember opening a present "from Santa" that was obviously a hardcover book. At that time, I believe I was going through my gory war period, and everything I borrowed from the local library was about warfare: biographies of war-famous generals, accounts of great battles, and even the odd Napoleonic volume or two. My favorite TV show was *Combat!*, a World War II drama that aired every Friday night.

So imagine my disappointment when I discovered that Santa's book was not about some bloody battle, but instead profiled the lives of Edwardian lady adventurers. Oh yawn! It was chapter after chapter of rather uptight, prudish-looking ladies trekking across the Gobi Desert or climbing the Himalayas, decked out in full corsets, bustles, bows and the most ridiculous-looking hats. These women would off-road across continents in open-top jalopies and Model Ts; their wind-burned, grimy faces stared back at me from the black and white photographs in the book, along with charts and maps that highlighted their expeditions, many of which were undertaken without male accompaniment and relied solely on Native guides for direction.

It wasn't until the following January that I finally looked at the book more closely, and after a few false starts, found myself drawn in to its stories of heroism and perseverance, of deprivation and loneliness and of the marginalization of women who chose to live outside the normal conventions of genteel domesticity.

There was a chapter about Mme Labrousse who, in 1899, became the first female race-car driver, entering the Paris-Spa race and finishing fifth. Complementing the story was a fuzzy photo of an elegant, well-dressed woman sitting astride a classic automobile, looking proud and determined. I remember thinking how exciting it must have been to be her. I read this during the '60s—a decade of great change for women around the world—and I think the seeds were planted then for my own future adventures. Either way, it contributed towards my love and appreciation of fast cars.

Even though I was living thousands of miles across the ocean in Australia at the time, I idolized legendary drivers such as Janet Guthrie, Lyn St. James, Pat Moss and even hot-rodder Shirley "Cha Cha" Muldowney, whose brilliant career and life story was told on-screen in the 1983 film *Heart Like A Wheel* (which I saw more for Beau Bridges, who I had a bad crush on).

During the '90s, motorsports' largest races with women competing took place in Europe, which seemed more willing to welcome female drivers to the circuits, unlike in North America where the super-macho mentality of NASCAR and Indy still reigned supreme. Finally, as the century drew to a close and we flipped our calendars over to a new millennium, we started hearing names like Erin Crocker, Danica Patrick, Melanie Troxel, Katherine Legge and Jutta Kleinschmidt being bandied about the track, all of whom are now competing at the highest levels of racing.

As the famous cigarette ad used to say, "You've come a long way, baby!" Yet there are still a few more miles to go; at least the ride is getting smoother and a heck of a lot more fun. So ladies.... start your engines!

THE PIONEERS

Chapter One

Anne-Cécile Rose-Itier

France

(1895–)

The Roaring Twenties was an age full of adventurous young women roaring around in their autos, in both North America and across Europe. One such fabulous flapper was the beautiful Madame Anne-Cécile Rose-Itier who, after escaping a bad marriage to a violent Scotsman, took up auto racing and flying aeroplanes in 1926.

Madame Itier got her first taste of four-wheeled competition in the Paris-Pau road race where she drove a Brasier auto. Throughout the rest of the decade, she entered mostly rallying and hill climb events; she won the 1928 La Mothe-Sainte-Héraye Hill Climb, and four years later found herself triumphant there yet again. Also in 1928, she hit the track for the Grand Prix Féminin at Montlhéry, considered by many to be one of the most presti-gious ladies' auto races of the day.

As the '30s dawned, she returned to circuit racing and competed in cyclecar events, which were the smallest major racing class. Cyclecars were tiny vehicles that were extremely quick, and as a result, the races were considered very dangerous, even for men. Rose-Itier drove her Rally SCAP model to some great finishes, including a fifth place in the Bordeaux Grand Prix in 1929 and a third in the Oranie Grand Prix. Over the first half of the decade, Madame Itier set about building her reputation behind the wheel of Bugattis, competing mainly in the smaller Voiturette class; but women were still thought of as second-class racers, more likely to crash than win. She was often disparagingly referred to as a "mobile chicane" by her chauvinis-tic competitors, but she eventually changed their opinion of her with her racing skills. In 1931, her first year in the Bugatti T37, she scored a seventh-place finish in the Tunisia GP, then placed fourth at the Circuit du Dauphiné and third at the Marne GP. In 1932, she scored her first win in the Trophée de Provence, improved to fifth in the Tunisian GP and captured fourth place at Casablanca. Her success continued through 1933, first with a victory in the Picardie GP in her T37 vehicle, then with a fourth-place finish at France's Albi track and a fifth-place finish in the Lemburg GP in Poland.

After switching to a Bugatti T51 in 1934, Anne-Cécile had to contend with as many disappointments as successes. She won the Phare Hill Climb and then came in third in the Picardie GP; but in the Eifelrennen at the Nürburgring, she only managed an eighth-place finish. She placed ninth shortly afterwards in the Swiss Berne GP, and although it was a big race, she was never forced to the back of the pack.

In 1935, Anne-Cécile and fellow Bugatti driver, Jean Delorme, founded the Union Sportive Automobile (USA) for independent drivers who didn't feel that they were being supported and protected by the established French Drivers Association (AGACI); the USA also helped increase the starting money fees for amateur drivers.

Madame Itier was a regular competitor at Le Mans from 1934 to 1938. She drove her first race in an MG Midget P, and she and her co-driver Charles Duruy placed 17th. In her second outing, she chugged in at 18th with co-driver Robert Jacob. In 1937, she made history by racing the first fully enclosed GT car at Le Mans. Unfortunately, her futuristic-looking Adler Trumpf failed to reach the finish line. She scored her best finish, a 12th place, in 1938 while driving an MG Midget Special.

As the possibility of a war in Europe drew near, Anne-Cécile returned to the rallying circuit even though she was starting to score some good results in the sports cars events. In 1938, she and co-driver Germaine Rouault placed third in the 12-Hours of Paris race, driving a Delahaye. Anne-Cécile also co-drove with Kay Petre in her Austin and often competed on the rally circuit with German driver Huschke von Hanstein. Anne-Cécile met Huschke when she was lost in a dust storm during the Moroccan rally and von Hanstein rescued her. This gallant man also won her heart, and for some time, the two were quite the romantic item on the racing circuit. It was behind the wheel of his Hanomag Diesel that Rose-Itier finished her last pre-World War II event, the 1939 Monte Carlo rally.

During the war, Madame Itier became a strong and brave underground heroine who helped evacuate children from occupied France, using her skills behind the wheel to out-drive her enemy pursuers. Once peace was restored in Europe, she resumed auto racing with renewed passion and fervor. She had little luck at first with her sports car outings in her aging Fiat Balilla, so she got herself a brand new Renault 4CV and promptly returned full-time to rallying.

She relaunched her rallying career by entering the 1948 Monte Carlo Rally with fellow '30s race-queen Hellé Nice as her co-driver, but unfortunately, they crashed and were unable to finish the race. Undeterred, Anne-Cécile kept racing every year until 1953, when she finally hung up her helmet for good at the age of 58.

Little is known about Anne-Cécile's final years apart from her continued involvement in administrating the USA organization until the early 1960s. What is well known, though, is that she was one of auto racing's pioneers, helping break down early gender barriers for all fast ladies of the future.

Chapter Two

Dorothy Levitt

United Kingdom
The Inventor of the Rearview Mirror

At the turn of the last century, women were often barred from taking part in motorsports as it was considered "unladylike," so many ladies who had a need for speed took up other forms of racing, such as in motorboats. This was the back door through which the legendary British speed queen Dorothy Levitt entered into the world of auto racing.

Little is actually known about this pioneer racer, and only one photo seems to exist along with a few press clippings. We do know that at the start of her career, she first worked as a secretary, and then took part in speed trials and long distance events wearing a distinctive long dust coat, hat and veil, which was generally required for ladies who drove.

Dorothy was competitive and won numerous motorboat races, including the first running of the Harmsworth Trophy in 1903; however, the record books reflect a different outcome. Mr. Francis Selwyn-Edge, her boss at the Napier Motor Company, took credit for the victory as the official owner of the winning boat, stating he hired Dorothy to skipper the vessel. That same year, Dorothy set the first World Water Speed Record, piloting her Napier-powered speedboat to 19 miles per hour.

Levitt began racing cars in between boat races, again under the guidance of Selwyn-Edge. Although not permitted on the main race circuits, women were allowed to compete in speed events and trials. This is where Dorothy excelled, winning her class at the Southport Speed Trial in a Gladiator auto. Few accounts of her races have been recorded, but by 1904, she had become the first female works driver to compete. She drove a De Dion auto in the Hereford 1000 Mile Trial and would most likely have won the gold medal if it hadn't been for a disappointing mechanical failure.

Then in 1905, she caused quite a sensation when she was chosen to drive an 80 horsepower Napier at the annual Brighton speed trials. There were many who didn't think she could handle the fast, heavy auto, but they had to eat their words (and her dust) when she won the prestigious Autocar Challenge Trophy.

Following her resounding success in Brighton, the French Mors team offered Dorothy the opportunity to drive in the Tourist Trophy race. This time, she would get to run a full race on a road course and was excited at the prospect, but Selwyn-Edge vetoed her participation, more interested in protecting his company's interest.

Dorothy made the history books yet again in 1906 when she set the Ladies' Record at the Shelsley Walsh Hill Climb, this time in a 50 horsepower Napier. It only took her 92.4 seconds to make it to the top of the hill, about 12 seconds shy of the overall winning time, but she knocked close to three minutes off the previous Ladies' Record set by Miss Larkins. Dorothy's record stood until 1913. The rest of the year wasn't all cheers and triumphs for her, though, as Dorothy endured several major disappointments throughout the season, including losing a famous challenge run against Freddie Coleman's powerful steam car.

By 1907, she had competed in all of the accessible time trials and hill climbs in England, so Dorothy crossed the English Channel to Europe and started proving her repute with a penalty-free run in Germany's exhausting Herkomer Trials. She won her first continental award there and then won her class at the Gaillon Hill Climb in France as a part of the winning Napier team.

Later that same year, Dorothy returned to England's newest race circuit, Brooklands.

Located in the county of Surrey, Brooklands was considered a racer's paradise. It had been built on an estate owned by Hugh Locke-King, himself a devoted racing fanatic. The track comprises an enormous concrete amphitheatre with a circular three-mile track and 30-foot-high banked corners. Until 1908, Brooklands' authorities would not permit women racers to compete and so, even though Dorothy had the full support of Selwyn-Edge and Napier, the Brooklands authorities wouldn't allow her to race. However, once the ban was dropped, women still encountered further indignities as they were forced to wear flowing silk scarves while driving in order to identify them-selves as women to race spectators.

Around 1908 Levitt's motorsport career stalled, although she maintained an active interest in the sport and published several books on driving, includ-ing her most famous volume entitled *The Woman and The Car*. In one chapter, Levitt recommends keeping a hand mirror in the tool drawer located under the driver's seat so that the driver, when necessary, would be able to see what was happening behind. Fortunately for us, her idea caught on and this was the genesis of what we now know as the rearview mirror.

The rest of her post-racing life remains shrouded in mystery, yet there is no doubt that Dorothy Levitt paved the way for Britain's future, more famous competitors such as Gwenda Stewart, Kay Petre and Pat Moss-Carlsson.

Chapter Three

Gwenda Stewart

United Kingdom

(1894–1990)

Born to Sir Frederick Manley Glubb, a celebrated soldier who served with distinction in World War I, Gwenda Mary Glubb also proved herself a worthy soldier by driving field ambulances on the Russian and Rumanian fronts while still in her early 20s. She transported wounded and dying soldiers to safety under horrendous conditions, and her dedication was rewarded with the Cross of St. George and Cross of St. Stanislaus medals.

While still in her youth, Gwenda trekked alone across the Canadian wilderness, wearing her hair and clothes in a masculine fashion so as to disguise her femininity. This adventurous spirit stayed with her all her life, through a number of marriages and through a series of two-, three- and four-wheeled racing formats.

Shortly after the end of the war, she married Sam Janson, who was her commanding officer in the war and, because of him, she started racing motorcycles. In 1922, riding a 249cc JAP-powered Triumph, she tore around the track at the famed Brooklands circuit, achieving an average of 44.65 miles per hour in an attempt to secure the Double 12-Hours record.

Gwenda then met and married Lt. Col. Stewart, and together they opened and operated a racing garage at Montlhéry in France near the Autodrome de Linas-Montlhéry, which was constructed in 1924 as an automobile racetrack and is located just outside of Paris.

Throughout the Roaring Twenties, she set records on both motorcycles and three-wheeled Morgan autos, and by 1931, she was renowned as one of the fastest people on three wheels. Behind the wheel of her sassy Morgan Aero, Gwenda set records for the standing and the flying kilometer at Montlhéry, which stood for many years and included the fastest speed ever recorded in a Morgan, a blazing 118 miles per hour.

In 1934 and 1935, she took on the grueling 24-Hours of Le Mans, driving a Derby 1100 auto on both occasions, and on August 6, 1935, Gwenda took the ultimate Brooklands Ladies Outer Circuit lap record at 135.95 miles per hour, beating Kay Petre's record set just three days earlier by a mere

0.65 seconds. Gwenda also set the outright record at Montlhéry in the Derby Special at 145.94 miles per hour. Although she often claimed that record-setting runs were more exciting to her than racing (and required less effort on her part), she was still nonetheless a quick and skilful racer.

As she competed throughout the 1930s, Gwenda seemed to prefer bigger, heavier cars such as the Derby or the Duesenberg, in which she completed the 500-Mile Race at Brooklands in 1935, scoring an impressive seventh-place finish. She also frequently drove with George Duller, a fellow British racer. The Stewarts parted ways around the middle of the decade, and in 1937 Gwenda again took a trip down the aisle, this time with Douglas Hawkes, who had a share in the Paris-based Derby auto factory that prepared Gwenda's Morgans and Derby-Millers for race day.

Although Gwenda proved her skill repeatedly on the open tracks, she was unfortunately over-shadowed by several of the other female racers of the era, drivers like Kay Petre. By the end of the '30s, her racing career was waning, and with the outbreak of World War II, she began working as a lathe operator in a munitions factory. After the war, she and her husband moved to the Greek islands, where they lived until Gwenda's death in 1990 at the age of 96.

Chapter Four

Kay Petre

Toronto, Canada

(1903–1994)

Toronto native Kay Petre, born Kathleen Coad Defries, was the daughter of a wealthy Canadian barrister whose clients included those living in both England and South Africa. The family eventually settled in England, a move that led to Kay's early visits to the famed Brooklands racing track.

Throughout the late '20s and into the '30s, Kay became a star, especially at Brooklands where the petite 4'10" driver was a media sensation, driving her huge 10.5 liter V12 Delage race car. Petre was always associated with the Delage, even though she started racing in a smaller vehicle, a Wolseley Hornet Special. She also frequently piloted an Invicta or a Bugatti, but she was most successful in a series of Rileys, placing ninth in 1934 at the Mountain Grand

Prix at Brooklands in her Riley 1.5. In August 1935, Petre raced against Gwenda Stewart in a duel for the Brooklands Women's Outer Circuit lap record. Petre had originally clocked an impressive 129.58 miles per hour lap on October 26, 1934, and she set a new record of 134.75 miles per hour earlier that day; but Stewart, driving her Derby-Miller, set the final record with a momentous run at 135.95 miles per hour.

That same year, Petre paid her first visit to Le Mans, where she and driving partner Dorothy Champney finished in 13th place, driving a Riley Ulster Imp. In 1935, she returned to Le Mans partnered with Elsie "Bill" Wisdom, but Petre's Riley let them down when a blown engine forced them to retire.

When Kay was successful on the track, the press went crazy for her. Not only was she fast, but she was also a fashion plate, adding glamour to the grime and sweat of serious auto racing. As a result, she was regularly featured in newspapers, which carried photographs of her kitted out in a tailor-made, racy, white leather jacket and helmet. Kay cut quite the figure both on and off the racetrack, and her skill and style were admired by both men and women.

During the mid-'30s, Petre competed regularly at all the big British races, such as the Brooklands 500-Mile Race and the Double 12-Hours, as well as in numerous other sports car events. She was often partnered with some pretty big names in racing, like Dudley Benjafield and Prince Bira of Siam. Also an accomplished rally and hill climb driver, she twice claimed the Ladies' Record at Shelsley Walsh.

Petre and her Riley auto traveled to South Africa in 1937 for the Grand Prix motor racing season, and it was there that she became friends with the legendary Bernd Rosemeyer, who was racing for Auto Union. She competed against all the top male drivers in three subsequent Grands Prix, scoring a sixth-place finish in the Grosvenor GP; unfortunately, she was not able to finish the other two races. Kay also traveled to France in September that same year and raced a Grasshopper Austin in the Paris-to-Nice rally.

Shortly afterwards, she was back in England as the works driver for the Austin Motor Company, and at Brooklands, Kay Petre's career and life were nearly ended by a horrendous crash. During her practice session for the 500-Mile Race, fellow driver Reg Parnell rear-ended her Austin Seven after severely misjudging a passing move. His car lost speed and went sliding down the banking, slamming into Petre, who sustained critical, life-threatening injuries. After a long recovery, she returned to Brooklands early in 1938 and spent time practicing in her Riley auto, but her passion was gone. She never raced competitively again.

Kay Petre withdrew completely from the world of auto racing and many years passed before she spoke about the sport and her crash. She eventually took up fabric design and created stylish patterns for the interiors of the swinging '60s iconic auto, the Austin Mini, as well as taking up freelance auto journalism for a while. She passed away in 1994 at the age of 91.

Chapter Five

THE BUGATTI BABES

Two legendary early women racers favored the Italian Bugatti auto, France's Hellé Nice and Elizabeth Junek of the Czech Republic. Both raced during the '20s and the '30s, and both led colorful lives of triumph and controversy.

I. Hellé Nice

Aunay-sous-Auneau, France

(1900–1984)

Hellé Nice was born Mariette Hélène Delangle in December, 1900 to Alexandrine and Léon Delangle, who was the local postman in their small village of Aunay-sous-Auneau, Eure-et-Loir, almost 50 miles outside of the city of Paris. Afraid that she too would be doomed to a life of boredom and anonymity like her older sister, who took over as village postmistress when their father died prematurely, the lively Mariette fled the family home at the age of 16 and headed into Paris. There she soon found work in the city's famous music halls.

Under the stage name Hélène Nice, she became a successful dancer and also modeled for fashion designers and artists during the heady days of the jazz age and flappers.

This was the era of Josephine Baker and her infamous "banana dance," and Hélène soon became known for her outlandish behavior and nudity. She craved the spotlight and attention of the male club patrons and surrounded herself with many great men of the time. Throughout her life, she had numerous affairs: with a married count and other members of the European nobility, with a famous wine baron, with well-known actors, and later, when she herself was racing, with other popular racing drivers.

After changing her name to Hellé Nice, she built a solid reputation as a solo dance act, and in 1926, Hellé decided to partner with Robert Lisset in order to perform in the major cabarets around Europe. She earned a small fortune from dancing and modeling, which enabled her to purchase a home and a yacht.

But sailing was just not fast enough for Hellé. During the '20s, Paris was one of the main centers for French auto manufacturing and offered many competitions and events for auto enthusiasts. Hellé loved the thrill of driving fast cars and longed to compete in one of the racing events held during the annual fair. The seed was planted and cars soon became the love of her life. Coupled with a downhill skiing accident that permanently damaged her knee and subsequently ended her dancing career, Hellé began to seriously contemplate switching to auto racing so as to not strain her damaged joint.

So as the jazz age declined, Hellé Nice decided to focus on professional auto racing, and in 1929, driving an Omega-Six, she won an all-female Grand Prix race at the Montlhéry racetrack, setting a new World Land Speed Record for women. To capitalize on her newfound fame behind the wheel, she toured the United States the following year, racing at numerous tracks in an American-made Miller racing car.

But Paris beckoned her home, and a short time after returning from America, while sitting at a café on the Champs-Élysées, the wealthy and powerful Philippe de Rothschild introduced himself to the glamorous speedster. They quickly became a couple, sharing both a bed and a passion for fast automobiles, and eventually de Rothschild introduced Hellé to Ettore Bugatti, the owner of the successful car company. Bugatti saw Hellé as the ideal feminine competitor to add to his roster of male drivers and so, after years of wishing to compete with the men, Hellé achieved her goal in 1931, racing a Bugatti T35C in five major Grands Prix in France as well as in the Italian Grand Prix at Monza.

Hellé was a standout on the tracks driving her bright blue Bugatti. She was fearless behind the wheel and eager to compete against any and all male drivers. But she always found a way to also employ her femininity, exciting the crowds wherever she raced. Apart from various appearance fees, she was also able to negotiate numerous commercial endorsements, and although she didn't ever win a Grand Prix race, she always proved herself a worthy and legitimate competitor, often finishing in front of many of the top male drivers of the day.

During the early '30s, Hellé was the only woman on the GP circuit, and she continued to drive Bugattis as well as Alfa Romeos, competing against all the greatest drivers, including Robert Benoist, Rudolf Caracciola, Louis Chiron, Luigi Fagioli and Jean-Pierre Wimille. Hellé not only drove in Grand Prix races, but she also participated in hill climb events and road rallies across

Europe, including the famous Monte Carlo Rally.

In September 1933, she was competing in the Italian Grand Prix at the Autodromo Nazionale Monza, a race that would become infamous as one of the most tragic races in GP history and in which three of the world's top racers—Giuseppe Campari, Baconin "Mario Umberto" Borzacchini and the Polish count Stanislas Czaikowski—were all killed in track accidents and crashes.

Journeying to Brazil in 1936, Hellé competed in two Grand Prix races and had an accident of her own. During the São Paulo GP, as she was slightly behind the first-place Brazilian champion Manuel de Teffé, a group of trackside delinquents tossed a bale of hay onto the track just as the drivers approached. Hellé's Alpha Romeo barreled into the straw at over 100 miles per hour; it flipped through the air and then crashed into the grandstand where several fans were killed and nearly 50 were injured. Hellé was thrown clear of the car and landed on top of a soldier who, by taking the full brunt of the impact, saved her from certain death; unfortunately, the young man died instantly. Hellé was also thought to be dead as she was slumped over and lifeless. She was taken to hospital and awoke from a coma three days later; she then underwent two months of convalescence. Because of her miraculous survival, Hellé became something of a national hero to the Brazilians, and many families even began naming their newborn daughters "Helenice" after her.

The following year, she attempted a comeback by competing back-to-back in the famous Italian Mille Miglia and in the Tripoli Grand Prix, both of which offered considerable cash prizes. But Hellé failed to secure financial backing and had to settle with competing in the Yacco Endurance Trials for female drivers at the Montlhéry track in France. She shared driving duties with four other women for 10 straight days and nights, successfully setting 10 driving records that stand to this day.

Over the next two years she competed in rally racing, but still hoped to rejoin the Bugatti team. But in August 1939, her friend and one-time lover, Jean Bugatti, Ettore's eldest son, was killed while testing one of the company vehicles. A month later, all European racing came to an abrupt halt when World War II erupted. In the middle of the German occupation of France, Hellé moved to the warmer climate of the French Riviera, and in 1943, she purchased a home in the city of Nice where she remained with one of her lovers for the remainder of the war.

After the end of the war, Hellé raced in the 1949 Monte Carlo Rally. While attending a large party organized to celebrate the return of auto racing, Monaco's favorite hero and multiple Grand Prix champion, Louis Chiron, suddenly lashed out and accused Hellé of being a Gestapo agent during the war. Such an accusation was especially dangerous at the time and could result in serious ramifications even without any proof or witnesses; simply being accused by someone as powerful and revered as Louis Chiron therefore made it practicaly impossible to dispute. The stigma it carried marked the end of Hellé Nice's professional racing career.

Her sponsors immediately dropped her, and her name and accomplishments were virtually obliterated from racing history books. Ostracized by friends and acquaintances, she was also abandoned by her lover, who even went so far as to steal a great deal of her money. Her career ruined and her money gone, Hellé was forced to accept charity from a Paris organization established to help former theatre performers through times of scarcity.

No facts of Chiron's accusation ever came to light, and recent research could not substantiate the charge: the official Gestapo records in Berlin confirm that Hellé Nice had never been an agent. Ironically, Chiron drove for the Mercedes Benz team, which the Nazis were using as an object of propaganda for their philosophy of racial superiority at a time when Chiron's Jewish colleague and rival René Dreyfus was refused.

Although Hellé Nice became one of the most colorful pioneering women of auto racing, successfully competing in more than 70 high-profile events, she sadly spent her final years in a filthy rat-infested apartment in the slums of Nice living under a fictitious name so as to hide from the shame of Chiron's unfounded accusations. She had been estranged from her family for many years, and when she died in 1984, she was penniless and completely forgotten by the rich and glamorous Grand Prix crowd.

Her body was cremated, thanks to the generosity of the Parisian artists' charity organization that had helped her before, and her ashes were sent back to the village of Sainte-Mesme where her parents were buried. Sadly, Hellé's name is not engraved on the family's cemetery memorial and few, if any, race fanatics find their way to this little graveyard to pay homage to a wonderfully gutsy girl.

Hellé Nice was a star both on and off the racetrack, always willing to pose for cameras; but she made too many enemies, especially with other women whose husbands she dallied with. Her off-track lifestyle enraged many people and even 40 years after her death, an aging rival still remembered Hellé bitterly during an interview: "I don't believe she ever thought about anything but sex and showing off." These days, it seems, that would be considered a badge of honor!

II. Elizabeth Junek

Olomouc, Moravia

(1900–1994)

Helle's contemporary, Eliška Junková (known to racing fans as Elizabeth Junek), was dubbed the "queen of the steering wheel" by the press and had a brilliant career driving Bugattis, the most luxurious and expensive cars in the world. She was the first woman to win a Grand Prix event and is regarded as one of the greatest female drivers in Grand Prix motor racing history.

Alzbeta Pospíailová came into the world on November 16, 1900, in the little town of Olomouc, Moravia, which was at the time part of the Austro-Hungarian Empire. Eliska (as she liked to be called) was the sixth of eight children born to her mother and father, a blacksmith, but sadly only three of her siblings survived into adulthood.

Nicknamed *smisek* for her constant smile, Eliska daydreamed of traveling the world, and by the age of 16, could speak fluent German and passable English, which helped her obtain a job in the Olomouc branch of a mortgage bank after she graduated high school. It was there that she met Vincenc "Cenek" Junek, an ambitious young banker who had been discharged from the army after being wounded.

Initially, they gave each other a wide berth, but when Cenek moved to the town of Brno to open another branch of the bank, he asked Eliska to go along with him. In Brno, Eliska began studying English and French formally, and when Cenek was reassigned to Prague, again she followed him. Love was blossoming.

In order to improve her language skills, Eliska decided to immerse herself in the French culture and went off to France on her own to work in a garden nursery. To do so, she had to delay her response to Cenek's numerous marriage proposals. Eliska wanted desperately to travel the world before she settled down, and her immediate plan was to see the North African deserts then to head for Ceylon (known today as Sri Lanka).

While making her way towards Gibraltar, Eliska was stopped by Spanish customs officers who wouldn't allow her to leave, so instead she ingeniously joined the kitchen staff of a British ship heading in that same direction. Unfortunately, she was denied a visa upon berthing in London, and Eliska was forced to return to France.

Cenek rushed to Paris to meet Eliska, but instead of a romantic reunion under the Eiffel Tower, they met up in a grimy auto shop. The young man had done well for himself during the early years of the Czechoslovak First Republic, and by 1921, he had amassed enough money to be able to better indulge his passion for fast cars.

Eliska also fell in love with sports cars, especially the luxurious Bugatti. In 1922, she and Cenek returned to Prague where Eliska secretly took driving lessons and Cenek started racing in earnest, winning the Zbraslav-Jiloviste Hill Climb that year. And finally, before the end of the year, Cenek and Eliska were married.

The couple began racing together in local events. Due to his wartime injury, however, Cenek had trouble shifting gears, and Eliska, who started out as his riding mechanic, took over the driving duties. At first they purchased a state-of-the-art Mercedes, but shortly afterwards, in 1923, Cenek gave his wife an Italian-made Bugatti Type 30 after a rather tough race that ended in triumph. The celebratory Bugatti henceforth became Eliska's trademark auto.

The Bugatti race cars may have been some of the most beautiful cars ever built, but they weren't perfect. In fact, the vehicles suffered from faulty, weak brakes. After he was criticized for the design of his braking system, Ettore Bugatti is reported to have uttered: "I build my cars to go, not stop." Ettore and Eliska became lifelong friends.

In 1924, Eliska took the wheel at Lachotin-Tremosna in Czechoslovakia, winning in the touring cars category, and became a national celebrity overnight. She then took first place in 1925 at Zbraslav-Jiloviste, after which the Juneks purchased yet another Bugatti, not only to celebrate but also because, from that year onwards, riding mechanics were banned on all the big-name European circuits, as they had been in America. Eliska and Cenek, forced to race as individuals, needed another car.

By 1926, Eliska was so good behind the wheel that she competed regularly in races throughout Europe against the era's best male drivers, and as she gained fame her name was anglicized to Elizabeth. That season, she was runner-up in the Klaussenpass in Switzerland then competed in the Targa Florio in Sicily, a race requiring great physical strength due to the nature of the rough and often muddy course. Being a gifted technical driver, Eliska is credited with being one of the first drivers to walk around a course before an event, noting landmarks and checking out the best lines through the corners.

She went on to win the two-liter sports car class at Nürburgring, Germany, making her the first and only woman in history to ever win a Grand Prix race. With such fame and celebrity, the glamorous Juneks were often gossiped about in the society pages. The burgeoning country of Czechoslovakia was looking for national heroes, and Eliska and Cenek fit the bill perfectly.

Planning for another win at the 1928 Targa Florio, Eliska acquired a new Bugatti Type 35B that would enable her to be on equal footing with her male competitors. By the end of the first lap, Eliska was in fourth place behind none other than Louis Chiron, in his own factory-sponsored Bugatti, and she was in the lead by the second lap. However, as the final lap approached, she ran into trouble when she spied two rocks in the middle of the road. The rocks had not been on the track during the previous lap, so it is easy to suspect that they were planted there to prevent a woman from winning. Eliska ended up finishing fifth, still better than 25 other top drivers, including the likes of Luigi Fagioli, Rene Dreyfus and Ernest Maserati.

Heading back to compete at Nürburgring in July of 1928, she shared the driving duties with Cenek at the German Grand Prix. She had just changed places with him when he suddenly went off course, crashed and was killed instantly, leaving Eliska completely heartbroken.

Devastated, she gave up racing and sold her vehicles, and after a period of intense mourning, she eventually returned to her first passion: traveling. Old friend Ettore Bugatti gave her a new touring car for her journey to Ceylon and hired her to research new business opportunities in Asia. But she never competed again, not even at the Brno Grand Prix, the pride of the new Czechoslovak nation. But with the communists taking over in Czechoslovakia, she was largely forgotten by the motor racing world. She did eventually find love again and remarried shortly after the end of World War II, but disapproving of her previous high-flying bourgeois lifestyle, the Communist authorities prevented Eliska from traveling outside of the country between 1948 and 1964.

Eliska lived well into her 90s, long enough for her to witness the fall of the Iron Curtain. In 1989, as she was nearing her 90th birthday, she attended a Bugatti reunion in the United States as the guest of honor. She made the journey against her doctor's advice, but the feisty pioneer racer would not be denied her long-awaited moment in the spotlight.

Eliska died peacefully in January of 1994, but her spirit lives on in Czech composer Jaroslav Jezek's classic 1928 jazz piece "Bugatti Step." Like Hellé Nice, her French counterpart, Elizabeth Junek's historic achievements in racing have only recently been given the recognition they deserve.

TRAILBLAZERS

Chapter Six

Louise Smith

Barnsville, Georgia, United States

(1916–2006)

Long considered stock car racing's "First Lady of Racing," Louise Smith was one of the true pioneers of early stock car racing, running Modifieds from 1946 through 1956.

Born in 1916 in Barnsville, Georgia, her family relocated to a farm near Greenville, South Carolina, when she was four. As a child, Louise experienced her first agony of defeat when she innocently hopped up behind the wheel of the family Model T Ford to play and accidentally released the brakes. She ended up gunning the truck right into the side of the chicken coop. The Model T and the coop were both wrecked, and her father was hopping mad, but this knack for surviving crashes would later prove to be a valuable asset throughout Smith's career.

The Georgia native started out helping Bill France Sr. promote the early pre-NASCAR races from Daytona to Canada, and although she was merely considered a novelty being a female driver, Smith's fearless style of driving made her an instant crowd favorite. Ever the consummate showman, France Sr. brought his races to Greenville in 1946 and decided to bring a woman in to race against the men; Louise fit the bill perfectly. She had allegedly outrun every lawman in the Greenville area, and although she had never even seen a race, much less been in a race car, Smith welcomed the opportunity to show off her driving skills.

On race day, she ended up finishing third driving a 1939 Modified Ford coupe and Smith's racing career was off to a flying start. And fly she did. Smith didn't realize at first that the checkered flag race officials waving madly as she passed the start line actually marked the end of the race, so she kept driving hard around the track while all the other drivers went to the pits. Around and around Louise went until someone remembered she had been instructed not to stop until she saw a red flag. Finally, a red flag was hastily brought out and Smith pulled her car to a stop. As she got out of her car the excited crowd cheered madly, but many of her fellow racers, all men, simply stood back and glared with disbelief and disdain. In a 1998 *Associated Press* interview, Smith told a reporter just how difficult it was for her competing in those early races:

"Them men were not liking it to start with, and they wouldn't give you an inch."

But she went on to prove that she wasn't racing just for show. Smith won 38 Modified races during her 11 years of racing, and from the tracks of New York to South Carolina and Alabama, she held her own against some of the greatest drivers in the sport, including legends such as Buck Baker, Curtis Turner, Fonty Flock, Red Byron, Roy Hall and Ralph Earnhardt. Louise Smith was a real racing barnstormer, often competing for first-place prize purses of $100 to $150 as well as earning any extra appearance money.

In 1947, under the ruse of going on vacation, she drove down to Daytona in her husband Noah's brand new Ford coupe to watch the races on the beach. She had hidden a special racing engine in the trunk of the car and when she reached Daytona, Smith had the car overhauled and entered the shiny new family car in one of the beach races. She drew the unlucky 13th starting position and halfway through the race, as she was approaching the north turn, she hit the back of a seven car pile-up, became airborne, flipped over and landed upside down. Several police officers patrolling the race rushed to her aid and turned her car over. Smith was fine except for a few bumps and bruises, so she continued racing and finished ironically in 13th place. This time, she welcomed the sight of the checkered flag.

Up to this point in her "career," she had managed to hide her racing habit from her husband, who was vociferously not in favor of women in the sport. Louise bought a bus ticket back home and concocted a cover story to explain the loss of Noah's car. Unfortunately, the local Greenville newspaper had carried a picture of her Daytona wreck, and the news was all over town before she even got home.

Louise was notorious for spectacular wrecks, and one particularly brutal crash nearly ended her life. During a race at Hillsborough, she pinwheeled her car into the air, and it took over half an hour to cut her out of the wreckage. Smith had four pins inserted into her knee and required 50 stitches to close all the wounds. Another time, at the Mobile racetrack, she dueled unsuccessfully with Fonty Flock and ended up sitting on the roof of her car in the middle of the lake.

Smith accumulated an impressive record of 38 wins on dirt tracks during her 11-year racing career driving Modified, Sportsman and Late Models. Eventually, all the men came to respect Smith's talented driving, even dubbing her the "Good Ol' Gal" of NASCAR. She was a true hard-charger with a passion for winning and had to fight for everything she gained. Legend has it that once she even pawned her diamond ring to spring her pit crew from the local jail after a post-race bar brawl.

Smith retired from racing in 1956 but remained active within the racing community, helping at tracks and even sponsoring cars to assist young up-and-comers like 1978's Rookie of the Year Ronnie Thomas. She and husband Noah never had children of their own, so she lent her support to many of the young drivers throughout the '70s and early '80s.

Louise Smith raced for the love of her sport. "Money was nothing back then," she admitted in the 1998 *Associated Press* interview, "We would have to put our money together just to split a hot dog and a Coke. I won a lot, crashed a lot, and broke just about every bone in my body, but I gave it everything I had."

In 1999, Louise became the first woman inducted into the International Motorsports Hall of Fame in Talladega, Alabama, and was a member of the Living Legends Racing Club in Daytona Beach, as well as the Old Timer's Racing Club in Archdale, North Carolina, and the Georgia Automobile Racing Hall of Fame in Dawsonville.

Louise Smith took her final checkered flag on April 15, 2006, dying at age 89 after a lengthy battle with cancer. She was buried in Greenville, where she had lived for most of her life.

Chapter Seven

Pat Moss-Carlsson

United Kingdom
(1934–)

Pat Moss-Carlsson ranks as one of the greatest women rally drivers in British history. The sister of another Brit racing legend, Stirling Moss, she competed throughout the 1950s and '60s and became the European champion in 1959. The following year, she won the Liege-Rome-Liege rally, which had never before been won by a British driver. Pat's co-driver for that race was Ann Wisdom (whose nickname was Whizz), a pair that had originally teamed up when they were both 18; Ann hadn't even passed her driving test when she started to navigate!

Pat had her first driving lesson at the age of seven, courtesy of her brother. Stirling had parked a Willys Jeep on the lawn, and he guided his sister around the flowerbeds and trees. The whole experience may have been "rather boring" for the little girl, but by the age of 13 or 14, she was competently driving the family's Land Rover around the farm, taking great delight in scaring all the chickens. But Pat's first love was horses, and she spent most of her childhood riding around the English country-side, show jumping and mucking out stables, a far cry from the greasy garages and racing pits that she would soon come to frequent.

Both of Pat's parents were race car drivers: her father used to race competitively and drove at Brooklands and Indianapolis, and her mother rallied and participated in hill climbs. Big brother Stirling was car mad and by the age of seven he already had an Austin 7 jalopy with two seats and virtually no body on top of the chassis.

It wasn't until she was 17 or 18 that Pat got her first taste of rally driving, when Stirling's manager, Ken Gregory, asked her to navigate for Stirling in a 1953 racing event. She thought it looked like fun and decided to give it a shot; after that, there was no looking back.

She got herself a Morris Minor, a small compact British car often referred to as a "granny-mobile," but try as she might, the power just wasn't there. Pat soon wanted something faster and sportier, and she eventually managed to buy a much sexier car, a Triumph TR2. She earned the money by selling the old Morris to her father, along with a half-share in one of her horses.

She competed successfully in the TR2 and was soon noticed by race fans and industry insiders. She was offered a drive in the Royal Automobile Club (RAC) Rally by the British Motor Corporation (BMC), who gave Pat a ride behind the wheel of their MG TF. For the following five years, Pat and her navigator Ann Wisdom competed around Britain and Europe for BMC, scoring some good finishes.

In 1958, the pair started enjoying major successes with two fourth-place finishes in the RAC and Liege-Rome-Liege rallies. The following season, the pair scored a second in the German rally and a creditable 10th on the Monte Carlo rally; and finally, in 1960 they scored their first win in grand style. The Liege-Rome-Liege was easily one of the most punishing endurance rallies in Europe, and the Austin-Healey 3000 was BMC's most demanding and difficult car to drive. This onerous combination did not seem to faze the two determined British ladies, and Pat drove the big car to a commanding victory.

Pat also enjoyed driving Mini Coopers, Ford Cortinas, Saabs and Lancias. She loved all of her cars and spoke about them as if they were human. She christened her Morris 1100 "Dirty Gerty" and named her Saab "Bloody Mary." The big

Austin-Healey was simply dubbed "URX" after its license plate.

Pat enjoyed a rather quiet race season in 1961 with a couple second-place finishes in the Alpine and RAC rallies; but in 1962, Pat experienced a dramatic turn of events. She was far from home, competing in the East African Safari rally for Saab, where she finished a respectable third. However, when she returned home, she was given the doleful news that Stirling had been seriously injured at Goodwood.

Pat spent many days fretting over her brother's injuries, but once he was out of danger, she got back behind the wheel of her BMC Mini and promptly won the Tulip rally. Pat then suffered another kind of loss when Ann Wisdom decided to retire in order to marry and start her own family. But once again Pat bounced back, this time hiring Pauline Mayman as her navigator. The new team went on to win the Baden-Baden Rally in Germany, again in the Mini. Pat and Pauline scored more great finishes in the Mini and the Austin-Healey, including a score of third places in the Geneva, RAC and Alpine rallies, as well as a second in the Polish rally. However, Pauline soon left and returned to the driving seat for BMC in 1963.

This wasn't the only big change for Pat in 1963; in June, she married Swedish multi-champion Erik Carlsson and the couple became teammates at

Saab, where Carlsson had been the leading driver for many years. Pat had met her famous husband on the world rally circuit, which back in those days was more like a circus than an organized sport, with groups of international drivers from Germany, Sweden, England and France all mingling with each other both on and off the circuit. One day, Erik had apparently passed her an apple through the Healey's car window and she had to crane her neck right up to see him, as he was 6'3" tall. As with Adam and Eve, it was love at first bite.

That year, Pat drove the Saab 96 to a third-place finish at the Acropolis rally and then placed fifth at the Monte. She changed over to a Ford to compete in the Targa Rusticana road rally back home in England, where she and navigator David Stone drove their bright yellow Anglia car to another victory. After that triumph, she took on a few more Ford works drives in a Cortina and Lotus Cortina.

As Pat continued at Saab for a second year, she scored an impressive third-place finish in the Monte Carlo rally with Sweden's Ursula Wirth-Fernstrom as her navigator and a second place in San Remo with British Val Domleo. Pat enjoyed modest success over the next few years before switching to the Lancia works team.

Pat scored her last big-time win at the Sestriere rally in 1968, then placed second again in San Remo, partnered with Liz Nystrom. She also got the opportunity to take her Fulvia auto to the legendary Targa Florio road race in Sicily, where she managed a solid 19th-place finish.

Pat had always been competitive, but despite the obvious urge to beat her brother, she never took up circuit racing because she found it "boring." But even the most boring race can easily result in disaster, even with a pro manning the wheel. Pat was driving at Solitude in Germany when she had a terrifying accident. She was stuck at the back of the pack with AC Cobras and all the bigger cars were up front. She managed to pass them all even though it was raining heavily, but she was going too fast, and she hydroplaned entering the last bend.

Her Healey ploughed into an unforgiving embankment that was lined with railway sleepers for safety and course retention. One of the rail sleepers pierced the front wheel and went through the passenger seat, violently turning the car end over end down the bank. Despite the seriousness of the accident, Pat's main concern was the recovery of the side screens from the Healey since good ones were so difficult to come by. Husband Erik, who had been watching from the sidelines, ran headlong down the embankment and pulled the side screens off in an effort to rescue his wife; but Pat, bloodied and bruised, was so angry that Erik was ruining the Healey that she gave him hell even as he was pulling her from the wreck.

Pat's career continued until 1975, and she scored numerous podium finishes and awards in a variety of ladies' events. But since the mid-1970s, Pat has been more focused on her family and her love of horses. After some 20-odd years of racing, she and Erik settled down to domestic life in England and had a daughter, Suzy.

The Carlsson family now only drives Saabs and Erik continues to work for the company in PR. Saab also sponsored their daughter, Suzy, in her show-jumping career. Although highly competitive in riding, Suzy has never shown an interest in auto racing and was even reluctant to get her drivers license until, like her mom before her, she realized she would be able to drive her own horse van to and from the stable.

In October 2005, it was reported that Pat was suffering with cancer, but her health thankfully improved enough for her to leave the hospital at the end of the month to attend a horseshow with her daughter.

Pat Moss-Carlsson's incredible rally racing career has been commemorated in toy cars manufactured by the British Corgi company. She was undeniably her country's favorite female racer as well as a part of rallying's greatest love story.

Chapter Eight

Shirley Muldowney

Burlington, Vermont, United States

(1940–)

People think it's easy because you drive in a straight line. What they don't realize is you've got to react in a hurry. The whole thing's over in just a little more than five or six seconds...if you're good.

–Shirley Muldowney

And Shirley Muldowney was that good. Going from a standing start to speeds in excess of 250 miles per hour over a quarter-mile straightaway in her Top Fuel dragster, she became one of the most successful drag racers in history. She also broke down gender barriers in the mid-'60s when the term "women's lib" was just starting to be heard. Shirley Muldowney became a rallying point for women around the world because she was doing more than just paying lip service to women's issues;

she was participating—and succeeding—in a sport in which men predicted she would fail. Muldowney proved beyond a shadow of a doubt that women can succeed anywhere and in any sport, including behind the wheel of a powerful and unpredictable race car.

This drag racing legend was born Shirley Ann Roque on June 19, 1940, in Burlington, Vermont, to parents Mae and Belgium Benedict Roque. Shortly after her birth, the Roque family, which included Shirley's older sister Linda, moved to Schenectady, New York, where her father worked as a taxi driver and a professional boxer while her mother worked in a neighborhood laundromat.

Nobody in the Roque family showed much interest in auto racing, and in fact, the future star of the quarter-mile straightaway was more interested in dressing up, dancing and dating than participating in sort of sporting pastime. By age 16, Shirley managed to convince her family that high school was just not for her, and she dropped out of Nott Terrace High and promptly married a young mechanic by the name of Jack Muldowney, who also happened to be a drag racer. This "gas'n'grease" way of life was at first foreign to Shirley, who did not even know how to drive a car when she got married.

But it didn't take long before the name Shirley Muldowney became synonymous with high-speed, Top Fuel Dragsters and a long list of world firsts and records. When she finally got her driver's license, the rest, as they say, is history!

To help ends meet, Shirley got a job in the classified advertising department of a local newspaper and spent much of her free time with Jack testing her skills as a street racer and learning more about the mechanical aspects of her car. In 1958, their son John was born, and although Shirley doted on the boy, she did not forget about her other four-wheeled "baby" parked out in the garage.

Shirley and Jack became more involved in drag racing in the early '60s, and it soon became a passion that afforded them a major life change. Shirley, for example, went from being newspaper clerk to being on the cover of her employer's Sunday magazine cover, waving out at the readers from behind the wheel of her favorite Corvette.

Up until 1964 she had competed in a number of different race cars, including a factory experimental car during the 1963 season. Although this was the era of the typical June Cleaver stay-at-home mum stereotype, Shirley thrived on beating the boys at their own game and had no intention of backing down from anyone, no matter how much resistance she encountered. Her fiery determination and, as some would say, utter stubbornness, forever changed the sport.

In 1965, after a protracted fight with drag racing officials and managers who did not want a "little lady" driving anything more dangerous than a family sedan, Muldowney finally earned her license to drive a gasoline-powered dragster under the auspices of the National Hot Rod Association (NHRA), the sport's largest sanctioning body. In doing so, she became the first woman to race in an NHRA professional category, and Shirley spent the next four years on the "match race" circuit—where two cars of equal, or matched, power and construction race the quarter-mile against each other under the clock—in the east and mid-west.

After overcoming this initial hurdle, Shirley's first dragster, powered by a supercharged Chevy engine, started winning races and earned her much acclaim in the media and, begrudgingly, from the other racers and sports professionals. This helped propel Shirley onto the national racing scene where she garnered magazine and newspaper stories along with a growing legion of loyal fans. It also prompted interest from Hollywood and eventually turned into the 1983 motion picture *Heart Like A Wheel*, which starred Bonnie Bedelia and Beau Bridges and focused on her controversial affair with Conrad (Connie) Kalitta, played with passion and jest by Bridges.

By 1971, cars were being specifically designed for drag racing, and due to their strange appearance and odd proportions (long, skinny front ends with a jacked-up rear), they were referred to as "Funny Cars." They were anything but funny, though, being powered by a 500 cubic inch purpose-built, all-aluminum, supercharged racing engine that burned nitro-methane fuel and with a tubular chassis and fiberglass body. They were dangerous and extremely difficult to drive. The NHRA had introduced the Funny Cars to replace the now-obsolete Top Gas class, and Shirley was now racing in her own Plymouth, frequently reaching speeds over 200 miles per hour and finishing the quarter-mile track in seven or eight seconds. At her first Funny Car race in Lebanon Valley, New York, she won the event.

Shirley soon expanded her racing schedule by entering her first national event in the International Hot Rod Association (IHRA) and winning the 1971 Southern Nationals race in Rockingham, North Carolina. The following season, she scored second place at the same race. Along the way, Shirley had also earned the nickname of "Cha Cha" due to the little wiggle her car would make at the start of a race and her signature hot pink paint scheme. However, she dropped the "Cha Cha" moniker by the end of 1973, after which she was quoted as saying, "There's no room for bimbo-ism in drag racing."

But glory did not come without a price, and in 1972, her marriage to Jack ended. Never one to allow personal issues to get in the way of racing, Shirley moved to Mt. Clemens, Michigan, to be closer to the Midwestern racing scene and spent three years behind the wheel of her Funny Car trying to extinguish the emotional pain leftover from her divorce. Physical pain was no stranger to Shirley either, as she was involved in several bad fires caused by engine parts failures.

Drivers of Funny Cars sit directly on top of the motor, which can cause massive fiery explosions. When the car is traveling at speeds well over 200 miles per hour, and if it crashes, the oil and fuel hit the red-hot exhaust pipes and ignite in milliseconds. Imagine racing directly into a blowtorch while traveling at a speed equal to one football field per second. One of Shirley's worst fires happened during the 1973 NHRA U.S. Nationals held at Indianapolis, but she soon recovered and bravely climbed back into the cockpit to race at the Cayuga Dragway Park in Ontario, Canada, where she made the switch from Funny Cars to the premier class of Top Fuel.

Top Fuel cars are designed with the driver's compartment just in front of the engine and are considered the world's fastest race cars. Shirley became the first woman ever to be licensed for Top Fuel competition in the NHRA after she successfully made numerous runs in the late Pancho Rendon's car. With legendary racers such as Don "Big Daddy"

Garlits, "TV Tommy" Ivo and Connie Kalitta (now all members of the Motorsports Hall of Fame, as is Muldowney herself) witnessing her license runs, NHRA had no choice but to issue Shirley her license, despite their reluctance to support a female driver.

She competed again in the U.S. Nationals in 1974 with her own car and race team, posting the top speed of the meet at 241.58 miles per hour. She also scored a semi-final finish at the National Challenge in New York State with an elapsed time of just over 6.09 seconds for the quarter-mile.

On June 15, 1975, she became the first woman ever to advance to the finals of the NHRA Spring Nationals in Top Fuel, but she lost the last round of racing to Marvin Graham. Two months later, on August 24, she caused a sensation when she became the first woman to break the five-second barrier. During the Popular Hot Rodding (PHR) Championships in Martin, Michigan, she blasted home with an elapsed time of 5.98 seconds. Only weeks later at the U.S. Nationals, she again advanced to the finals. This time, however, she came up short against Don "Big Daddy" Garlits. But her season-long accomplishments earned her a place on the prestigious 10-member "All American Team" as nominated by the AARWBA (American Auto Racing Writers & Broadcasters Association).

Next season at the Spring Nationals, she qualified in first position with a 6.09 second performance, then posted the lowest elapsed time of the race (5.96 seconds) and the top speed of the event (243.90 miles per hour). Shirley Muldowney finally won her first NHRA national event on June 13, 1976. She won her second race of that season while competing at the World Finals in Ontario, California, on October 10, 1976, by posting the lowest elapsed time (5.77 seconds) and the top speed (249 miles per hour). These were the fastest runs clocked in the entire 1976 season, and despite only racing in four of the eight NHRA national events, Shirley scored a 15th-place finish for the season, was voted Top Fuel Driver of the Year by *Drag News* magazine and was chosen once again as a member of the "All American Team" by the AARWBA.

Shirley thrived on the match race circuit and enjoyed getting the hefty appearance fees handed out by track operators for her to race against other hired-in male competitors. These so-called "Battle of the Sexes" races were a great ticket-selling promotion, especially as Muldowney had a reputation for rarely pulling any punches. Many a pre-race interviewer found himself "refereeing" Shirley's crowd-inflaming commentaries, which led to even greater drawing power.

With so much momentum going into the 1977 season, Shirley knew this would be her biggest year ever, and she didn't have long to wait before she entered the history books by becoming the second person ever to run over 250 miles per hour. On January 17 at a race in Arizona, she posted a speed of 250.69 miles per hour and then drove a blazing 252 miles per hour during qualifying. She then posted at 253 miles per hour during the Winston World Series event on May 7 in Irvine, California. In June at the NHRA Spring Nationals in Columbus, Ohio, she won the race for the second straight year, and at the next event, she qualified number one. She went on to post two more number-one finishes that year—on July 10 at the NHRA Summer Nationals in Englishtown, New Jersey, and on August 7 at the NHRA Molson Grand Nationals in Canada—and on August 14, Shirley scored a runner-up finish at the PHR Championship in Martin, Michigan, beating rival Don Garlits along the way.

Her phenomenal accomplishments won her the 1977 Winston World Championship for points in Top Fuel, making Shirley Muldowney the first and only women ever to do so. So monumental were these achievements that on October 14, the United States House of Representatives bestowed her with the "Outstanding Achievement Award." *Drag News* magazine proclaimed her the Top Fuel Driver of the Year for the second consecutive season and *Car Craft*, one of the nations most prestigious publications, anointed her Person of the Year.

Shirley had another banner year in 1980 with wins at the Winter Nationals, the Spring Nationals, the Fall Nationals and the Winston World Finals. At the time she was the only driver in the sport to ever win two Winston Points Championships in Top Fuel. What made that win even more impressive was her second-place finish in the AHRA Top Fuel wars in the same season, thereby nearly clinching two titles simultaneously!

During the following season, Muldowney concentrated her racing efforts on winning the AHRA title, which she successfully brought home. This gave her two Top Fuel titles in two successive seasons while also finishing in the top five for NHRA that year.

In 1982, Shirley set her sights back on the NHRA and scored big time. She became the first professional driver in Top Fuel to win the World Championship three times in a career. She was voted to the *Car Craft* All-Star Team as Top Fuel Driver of the Year for the second consecutive season and voted to the AARWBA top 10 for the fifth time, receiving the highest number of votes ever by a driver.

The next year, she finished fourth in Winston Points with landmark wins at the Winter Nationals and the World Finals championships. Then at Columbus, Ohio, one of her favorite tracks, she went to the finals for a record six times in eight years. After 25 years in drag racing, one would think that Shirley had seen and done it all, fighting off all-comers just to get into racing, yet 1984 would present her with one of her biggest and most terrifying battles yet.

On June 29, 1984, a front tire failure on her fuel dragster caused a high speed crash at over 250 miles per hour that nearly ended her life. Her legs were badly broken and required five extensive surgeries. The bones in her left foot have been fused so much that her left leg is a full inch shorter than her right. Many people doubted she would ever walk again, let alone race, but there was no doubt in Shirley Muldowney's mind. Eighteen months later, after a painful recovery, she was back in a race car.

Shirley's fans had reached out to help with her overwhelming medical expenses, and shortly afterwards, the Drag Racing Association of Women (DRAW) was formed, which now continues to help the families of anyone injured in drag racing competition.

It would take nearly three long years before Shirley returned to her winning ways. In 1986, the AARWBA recognized her with the "Comeback Driver of the Year" award as she progressively fought her way back to top racing form. In 1988, love also found its way back into Shirley's life when she married Rahn Tobler, her crew chief and longtime friend.

By 1989, Shirley had returned to the thick of the Top Fuel wars, finishing in the top 10 of the Winston Points Championship. She advanced to the final round in NHRA competition three times that year, won the Fall Nationals and entered the Cragar Four Second Club with a run of 4.974 seconds at 284 miles per hour, the only woman to do so at that time.

Even though Shirley was still finishing in the NHRA top 10, she decided to switch gears for the 1991 season and returned to the match racing circuits where she had earned her stripes early in her career. Throughout the early part of the decade, Shirley competed in numerous match-racing schedules across the United States as well as overseas. In 1993, she set a track record of 5.30 seconds at 285 miles per hour at the Fuji International Speedway in Japan. Shirley actually set 12 new speed records at various facilities all across America and the world.

By 1995, her desire for high-profile competition brought Shirley back to the IHRA. In 1996, she reached the final round in International Hot Rod Association competition five straight times and won three national events back-to-back. She qualified in the top three at every race and finished the year in the number two spot for Top Fuel points.

Shirley continued running open competition in 1997 whenever her busy match-racing schedule allowed. In open competition, she set and re-set the highest miles per hour mark for the national record four times with a standing mark of 303.71 miles per hour. She held the number two spot in points, but decided not to go to the final race of the year, which dropped her back to a third-place finish for the season.

The high point of her year was being honored by the United States Sports Academy's 25th anniversary CNN/USA Today balloting for Top Athletes of the Past 25 Years. Names were presented in four categories for persons whose noted accomplishments have made an impact on their respective sports. In auto racing, Richard Petty of NASCAR fame was chosen as the Top Man, and Shirley Muldowney was chosen as the Top Woman, her dedicated 40 years of hot rodding having carved out an unmistakable niche in auto racing history.

Shirley had another successful season in 1998, setting track records for top-speed or elapsed-time at Atco, New Jersey, Milan, Michigan, Epping, New Hampshire, and Stanton, Michigan, where she not only engraved new track records but set a new performance record for the IHRA. Her 4.69 seconds at 312.50 miles per hour run during qualifying at the Northern Nationals was the quickest and fastest ever recorded in the history of competition, which proved once and for all what she was made of—pure speed.

Shirley was also granted one of the highest distinctions of her career when she was honored by the New York State Senate as one of Thirty Women of Distinction, and she was also part of a historical display presented at the state capital in Albany. Her historical motor sports accomplishments were acknowledged alongside such New York State luminaries as Susan B. Anthony and Eleanor Roosevelt.

Moving into the 21st century, Shirley Muldowney continued racing on the match-race trail where she still had a major draw, but a lack of critically important sponsorship kept her national outings to just a few. But thanks to backers like Goodyear, Action Performance and Mac Tools, Shirley was able to end her active driving career with the "Last Pass" tour, through which she continued to compete for the 2003 season. She finally retired at age 63—few sports support such career longevity—and her fans crowded the tracks to bid her farewell.

In 2005, Shirley published her memoir *Shirley Muldowney's Tales From the Track*, co-written with Bill Stephens, in which she chronicles her groundbreaking entry into racing and the pressures of being such a high-profile role model and competitor in a male-dominated sport. In the book, Shirley acknowledges how tough she had to be, stating that a hard-nosed man is "driven and aggressive," but the same type of woman usually gets tagged as a "bitch."

Never one to mince words, she says, "Yeah, I took the hits as a woman first coming into the sport, but I was perfect for that. I'm respectful and even kind, and I can be presentable in public, but my style works for me and the sport now seems to accept me." And as if to prove this, in March 2006, the "First Lady of Drag Racing" was inducted into the International Drag Racing Hall of Fame. On the subject of the new crop of women racers, she says wryly, "Girls seem to come and go in this sport; I'd like to see some longevity out of some of them. I did it when it was hard to do; no one handed me a ride."Throughout her distinguished racing career, her son John was never far from her thoughts, and thanks to a team of nannies and other caregivers, she was able to combine racing with a hands-on motherhood. During his childhood, John was always present at her race meets and now works as a fabricator.

For all her notorious thick-skinned hardness, Shirley Muldowney has lots of soft spots, including one for animals, and in particular, her own pets. She feeds and cares for three wild cats that wander around her property in Armada, Michigan, and owns two Chihuahuas named Peanut and Midnight. She admits to having a dream of running a home for abused animals once she steps completely away from the racing life....Dream on, Shirley!

Chapter Nine

Bunny Burkett

West Virginia, United States

(1945–)

America's Queen of the Funny Car

For over 40 years, Carolyn "Bunny" Burkett has helped shape the face of Funny Car racing and has become a symbol of determination, courage and inspiration, having survived both a near-fatal crash as well as breast cancer and overcoming a multitude of disabilities.

Born in 1945 in the hills of West Virginia, Carolyn Ruth Hartman moved with her mother and step-father to Chantilly, Virginia, when she was 13. Her mother operated a boardinghouse for the workers who were building the new Dulles Airport, and one of those boarders was a young man by the name of Mo Burkett. He and Carolyn started dating when she was 15, and their early romantic encounters were spent driving around on the par-tially built runways of Dulles. On their very first date he drove the impressionable young girl around the country roads at 145 miles per hour, and that night Carolyn fell in love with both the man and with speed. Mo taught her how to drive fast in his 1955 Mercury that once belonged to an ex-revenuer and was capable of hitting over 150 miles per hour. He even taught her the dangerous bootlegger turns.

The couple often attended drag races at the Old Dominion Speedway in Manassas, Virginia. Carolyn thought that drag racing was the most exciting thing that she had ever seen and realized that she would have to race some day. When she told Mo of her plans, he was not convinced that his young girlfriend was serious; Carolyn didn't even have her driver's license yet!

The pair married when Carolyn turned 16, and a year later they welcomed their first child, a beautiful daughter; however, after the initial excitement of motherhood had dimmed, she realized that she still wanted to race. One Thursday when she was 19, Carolyn and Mo purchased a 1964 Mustang, and just 24 hours later she was not only driving the car at Old Dominion, but she actually won her first race.

During these early days, she supported her hobby doing part-time clerical work for a friend and earning $85.00 a week, which left her free to race over long weekends. She was a regular competitor at famous East Coast tracks like Budds Creek and Aquasco, and during one period she won 22 of 23 races she entered, an astounding achievement by any standards.

Not only was Carolyn adding to her trophy collection, she also added another daughter to the family, and the Mustang she raced in on weekends also served as the family's daily transportation. Unfortunately, when the car was rear-ended and destroyed by a drunk driver, the Burkett's had no insurance to cover the loss. Not one to sit back and feel sorry for herself, Carolyn knew she had to bring in some more money, so she took a job working as a hostess in the Playboy Club in Baltimore. The money she earned went towards buying a new car, and she saw the famous bunny club as a fun and classy way to earn quick money. She often joked that all she had to do at work was "push 'em up and smile." She hopped around in a bunny uniform for almost a year and saved nearly $4000 in cash for a new 1967 390-powered Mustang. As soon as she took ownership of the car, she quit the Playboy Club to resume her fledgling racing career, and in recognition of her racing aspirations, Carolyn's friend Nelson Grimes painted "Lead Foot Bunny" on the back of her car; the name stuck. Ever since that day, Carolyn has been known as "Bunny" Burkett.

She soon got bored with the 390 and replaced it with a larger 427 cid Ford engine with dual carburetors, and soon she was running 10 flats at 140 miles per hour. Always on the lookout for ways to improve her speed, Bunny sold that Mustang and bought a 1973 Ford Pinto that was configured as a Jr. Pro/Stocker. Bunny's Pinto was always at the tracks, and she had her first accident in the car when she crashed at Roxboro, North Carolina. The parachutes used to help brake the car had somehow gotten wrapped around the wheelie bars, which triggered a barrel-rolling crash. When the rescue crew arrived to get Bunny out of the car, all they heard from her was, "Did I win?" to which the dumbfounded track official was reported to answer, "Yes, lady, you sure did!"

Bunny knew she would still need to come up with more money to feed her racing habit since poor Mo couldn't support the entire family as well as Bunny's career. She decided to take a position with an office supply company, and by applying the same determination to her work as she did toward racing, it wasn't long before she found herself working her way up the chain of command, ending up years later as the vice president of the company.

The little Pinto was eventually repaired and Bunny continued to race it for three more years. Despite it being a notoriously difficult car to drive,

Bunny was able to sweet-talk 9.30 seconds at 160 miles per hour out of the mechanical beast. When she heard that her old buddy Tom Smith was looking for alcohol-burning funny cars for a series of match races that he was promoting featuring other women drivers, calling it "The Miss Universe of Drag Racing Series," Bunny traded the Pinto in for a Mustang II Funny Car rolling chassis. She then traded in the Mustang for a sexy 1981 pink Corvette, then acquired a new 'vette in 1984, which launched a string of alcohol racers that Bunny continues to race today.

In 1986, Bunny and her team decided to go full force into racing, and soon a local speed shop owner came on board and the team ordered a brand new Dave Uyehara car and a Brad Anderson engine. With her win at the IHRA event at Darlington, the team started chasing the points, and after a successful season, Bunny became the first ever IHRA female Funny Car World Champion. She ran an almost perfect season on the NHRA tour that same year, winning the Keystone Nationals and the NHRA Division II season title, but Bunny had to settle for a respectable fourth in the NHRA national championship.

She also realized that it was becoming too tiring to maintain such a busy schedule with her family obligations, racing and three days a week at the office; so Bunny chose her family and her racing, giving up the vice presidency that she had worked 18 years to achieve.

From 1988 onwards, Bunny and her team spent their time match racing at tracks without having to pay to use the facilities and only occasional ventured into national event competition. But on Labor Day 1995, her life hung in the balance when she was involved in a horrendous car crash at the Beaver Springs Dragway in Pennsylvania.

She was racing against longtime friend Carl Ruth when he accidentally crossed over into her lane, speeding along at over 200 miles per hour. Ruth hit Bunny's car in the rear end and sent her careening over 100 feet into the woods alongside the track. By the time the emergency rescue crews got to the crash site, Bunny was unconscious; all of her arms and legs were broken as well as several of her vertebrae. On the way to the hospital, she had to be brought back from the brink of death three times.

Diligent surgeons worked on Bunny for nearly 39 hours, and family and friends waited seven days to learn whether she would live or die. But her determination and competitive spirit pulled Bunny through the ordeal, and following three weeks of comatose inactivity, Bunny started to bounce back. She spent the next nine months paralyzed and couldn't do even the simplest of tasks.

After several more months undergoing intensive physiotherapy, Bunny was finally able to walk again and could handle some light desk work, even driving her empty truck and trailer to the track to sell souvenirs to raise money for another race car. But Bunny quickly became bored of the slow life and started begging her doctors and her husband to allow her to get back on the track; it was time to get back on the throttle. A year and a half later, defying all odds and a reluctant husband, Bunny was racing again.

In the spring of 1997, even with some permanent disabilities and partial paralysis, Bunny passed a blindfold test proving that she still knew her way around a driver's compartment; a 228-miles-per-hour pass showed that she could still reach the finish line too. After impressing everyone with her recovery, she was finally released to drive again and was soon back in the seat of her Funny Car at the Virginia Motorsports Park making a pass down the eighth-mile.

With the support of her team, she raced a limited number of events over the next half-dozen years, and each time she turned up at a racetrack the fans went wild for Bunny. In mid-2006, Bunny was dealt yet another devastating blow when she was diagnosed with two types of breast cancer. She had undergone her annual mammogram in March, and by August, Bunny had already undergone a double mastectomy and endured months of doctor visits, numerous tests and a real quick education on the types of treatments available for breast cancer. Since surviving the cancer, Bunny now makes it her mission to stress the importance of annual mammograms to her fans and to women everywhere.

Phoenix-like, the incomparable Bunny rose up from the ashes of yet another near-disaster, making an amazing comeback on Sunday, October 22, 2006, when she drove her car onto the Maryland International Raceway for the Ford Fever Classic. Piloting her brand new 2006 Dodge Avenger Top Alcohol Funny Car down the MIR quarter-mile, her very first pass resulted in a 5.99 ET on the scoreboards at 240 miles per hour. Bunny was back….again!

Xena couldn't hold a candle to this warrior princess whose spirit refuses to allow her battered body to become an obstacle in pursuing her life long passion of drag racing.

Chapter Ten

Janet Guthrie

Iowa City, United States

(1938–)

Born in Iowa City, Iowa, Janet Guthrie made history by becoming the first woman to race in both the Indy 500 and the Daytona 500. These were classically macho races that had always been man's domain even during the World War II era, unlike other sports such as baseball; remember the film *A League of Her Own?* Janet had to race in cars that were entered simply to fill out the field—like the 20 to 1 long shots in a horse race—and the records she compiled in these "loaner" cars stands as a tribute to her true racing abilities.

When she was three, Janet's family moved to Miami, Florida, where she attended Miss Harris' Florida School for Girls during her teenage years. She graduated from the University of Michigan in 1960 with a Bachelor's of Science in Physics and eventually joined Republic Aviation in Farmingdale, NY, as a research and development engineer. She worked on programs akin to the famous Project Apollo, and in 1964, she applied for the first Scientist-Astronaut program, managing to get through the first round of eliminations. She received her pilot's license at age 17 and became a pilot and a flight instructor, as well as holding a post as a technical editor and a public representative for some of the country's major corporations. Janet also managed to chalk up 13 years of experience in sports car road-racing circuits, building and maintaining her own race cars and even being invited to test a car for Indianapolis.

From an early age, Janet was known as a bit of a daredevil and began racing Jaguars while working as an aerospace engineer in the 1960s. She first purchased a Jaguar XK 120 coupe and began competing in field trials and hill climbs, which then led to her purchase of another Jaguar, this time the more powerful XK 140 for competition in Sports Car Club of America (SCCA) races. In 1964, she won two SCCA races and finished sixth at the Watkins Glen 500. Going into 1971, she scored nine consecutive top-10 finishes in endurance races. Janet's career in physics was slowly occluded by the sheer thrill of sports car racing; by 1972, she was racing full-time and soon notched up two class victories in the 12-Hours of Sebring.

Guthrie passed her rookie test at Indianapolis in 1976 but ultimately failed to qualify. Instead, she switched race cars and took on the NASCAR World 600, finishing 15th. She was noticed by car owner Rolla Vollstedt, who put her behind the wheel of his car for the 1977 Indy 500, at the time the most prestigious event in American auto racing. Unfortunately, mechanical problems ended her race early on lap 27.

Undeterred, Guthrie returned to Indy the next year and finished in ninth place, officially the highest finish for a woman at the Indy 500 until it was topped in 2005 by rookie Danica Patrick, who finished fourth. Guthrie also drove a stock car in the 1977 Daytona 500, finishing in 12th place and taking top rookie honors in five NASCAR Grand National events. She was ranked third in voting for the Rookie of the Year Award.

In her brief but illustrious career at racing's top level, Guthrie earned top-10 starting positions and posted top-10 finishes in both Indy-car championship racing and in the NASCAR Winston Cup (now known as the Nextel Cup). Her final major race appearance was a fifth-place Indy-car finish at the Milwaukee 200 in 1979. Her sixth-place Winston Cup finish at Bristol in 1977 remains the best performance by a woman in NASCAR's super speedway era, and she was also the only woman to lead a Winston Cup race. Guthrie has often said that her greatest triumph, though, was her gradual acceptance by the male drivers on the NASCAR and Indy-car circuits. She won their respect by out-qualifying racing greats such as Bill Elliott, Ricky Rudd, Richard Petty, David Pearson, Bobby Allison, Neil Bonnett and Johnny Rutherford at the Talladega 500 in 1977. She finished ahead of Bill Elliott in 7 out of the 10 races in which they both competed and qualified higher than Dale "The Intimidator" Earnhardt two out of the three times.

Keeping a low profile in her private life, she kept her focus on the sport of auto racing. Throughout the mid to late '70s, she owned, managed and raced her own team car and also found time to get married in 1989.

Janet Guthrie retired from racing in 1983 and wrote her autobiography, *Janet Guthrie: A Life at Full Throttle,* which was eventually published in 2005. Her helmet and driver's suit are now on display at the Smithsonian Institution and she is a charter member of the Women's Sports Foundation's International Women's Sports Hall of Fame. Guthrie was inducted into the International Motorsports Hall of Fame in 2006.

Even though she is now almost 70, she has still not put on the brakes. Ms. Guthrie does extensive public speaking and has made frequent television appearances on *Good Morning America* to discuss the state of the sport and women's issues.

When once asked by a reporter to sum up her years of competition and how being a woman may have impeded her progress, she said quite matter-of-factly, "Racing is a matter of spirit not strength." And Janet Guthrie's spirit still has a strong influence on many of the women drivers entering the sport in the 21st century.

Chapter Eleven

Lyn St. James

Willoughby, Ohio, United States

(1947–)

When most women of a certain age are think-ing about hot flashes and mood swings, this legendary fast lady climbed into a race car and completed her first Indy 500. At the age of 45, Lyn St. James became the second woman in history to race in the prestigious event. Then eight years later, she made the record books once again by being the oldest driver to grid at the 2000 Indy 500. Lyn St. James' career has been fueled by unlimited determination and a real passion for the sport. She has risen through the ranks to become an icon of women's auto racing and is one of the greatest role models for young women with a yen for racing.

Born Sandra Lynn Eden in Willoughby, a suburb of Cleveland, to Alfred and Maxine Eden, she came into the world while the U.S. was still recovering from World War II. Alfred was a sheet metal worker and Maxine remained at home to care for the youngster as a traditional homemaker. Her mother suffered from childhood polio and as an adult was reliant on cars for mobility. This gave a young Lyn an appreciation of the freedom and independence that automobiles could provide. Lyn also spent a great deal of time with her father in his metalwork shop, learning the intricate workings of various machines and engines.

Lyn maintained her passion for cars throughout her life, and although she still loved to get greasy and mucky in the garage, she honored her mother's wishes and received a good education. Her parents enrolled her in the St. Andrews School for Girls, and she majored in business. She also earned a certificate in piano teaching from the St. Louis Institute of Music.

When Lyn was 17, she and some friends attended a series of drag races in Louisville, Kentucky, where one of the boys in her group of friends entered his GTO car in a race and was promptly trounced. After some serious teasing from Lyn, the young man suggested she put her car where her mouth was; so she hopped behind the wheel, and to everyone's amazement, blew away the competition and won her class. The seed was planted.

During a 1966 visit to the Indianapolis 500 event, Lyn managed to get racing star A.J. Foyt to autograph her race program, and from moment on the excited teen set her sights on a professional career in racing.

A few years later, Lyn fell in love. His name was John Caruso, and he was a Florida businessman who owned an electronics company. John was also a car nut, and soon he and his bride were competing in regional Sports Car Club of America (SCCA) amateur racing events in their Ford Pinto. They also bought an auto parts business, and Lyn felt right at home, just like she had when she was a kid working alongside her dad back in Cleveland.

John graduated to Corvette racing, and by default, Lyn kept campaigning in the Pinto. In 1976 and 1977, she was named the SCCA's regional champion. Her husband competed in the famed 24 Hours of Daytona while Lyn worked on his pit crew, but the experience left her feeling empty—she knew that she should be the one behind the wheel, not the one changing them.

Lyn decided she needed to maintain her own identity separate from that of her husband and their mutual business interests, and so being a fan of the Rock Hudson, Susan Saint James hit TV series *McMillan and Wife,* she chose the last name of "St. James" as her professional pseudonym. Unfortunately, as her career took flight, Lyn's marriage hit the pits, and within a year, she had divorced John Caruso.

Her first professional year of racing was 1979, and Lyn made an impressive entrance into the sport with a historical run in the (AIMSA) American International Motor Sports Association's Challenge Series; she finished in second place, only .079 seconds behind the winner.

The Ford Motor Company had been watching Lyn for quite some time, and in 1981, they decided to sponsor Lyn's racing. With the security of financial support behind her, she was able to compete in several race series, garnering the respect of fans and the media alike. In 1984, St. James was awarded the IMSA Camel GT Rookie of the Year honors, and the following year with her first professional win at Elkhart Lake, Wisconsin, she was presented with the IMSA Norelco Driver of the Year laurels.

Over the next five years, Lyn's name was entered into numerous record books. As a GTO team driver, she won the 24 Hours of Daytona in both 1987 and 1990, and in 1991, she took the 12 Hours of Sebring. She also raced in the legendary 24 Hours of Le Mans in 1989 and 1991. In 1988, she changed over full-time to Indy cars and was nominated for the Women's Sports Foundation Sportswoman of the Year Award.

After being dropped by Ford in 1991, St. James developed her own racing business, Lyn St. James Racing. Then in 1992, she finally heard the siren's call: "Gentlemen and lady, start your engines" at the Brickyard—she was driving in the world-famous Indianapolis 500! Although she only logged an 11th-place finish, she was still just the second woman in history to start the event, and St. James was rewarded at the end of the season with the Indy 500 Rookie of the Year award.

In 1993, Lyn fell in love again, marrying Roger Lessman with whom she had a daughter, Lindsay. For the next six seasons, Lyn made the starting grid at Indy. In 1994, she qualified in sixth place, the highest-ever qualifying position for a woman and a record that stood until 2005, when Danica Patrick qualified in fourth place. In 1995, she set a world record for women's closed-course racing when she clocked a sizzling 225.722 miles per hour during the Indy 500 qualifying session. She then developed a successful relationship with Lifetime Television, which sponsored her car from 1996 to 1998.

Lyn was as active off of the racetrack as she was on it. In 1994, she established the Lyn St. James (LSJ) Foundation, which is dedicated to providing education and leadership programs to up-and-coming young women racers. Lyn also made sure that she was accessible to fans at each and every event. Her amiable manner with the press and the thousands of fans who lined the tracks made her 1997's third most popular driver as voted by IRL fans.

She then became involved in the promotion of women's sports, and in 1999, she co-founded the Women's Global Series, which showcased the talents of women drivers. She also served as Chairwoman of the Women's Sports Foundation Governance Committee as both member of the organization's board of trustees (1988–93) and as president (1990–93).

Heading into the new millennium, St. James started to focus more on the business side of motor sports and became a motivational speaker. She raced fewer events, but made sure she gridded for the legendary 2001 Goodwood Motor Circuit Revival Meeting in England alongside other auto racing legends. Lyn St. James finally retired from the Indy circuit in 2001 at the age of 54. At the Indy 500, she took two ceremonial laps before the start of practice then pulled into the pits amid the cheers and tears from the thousands of fans in attendance as well as from her fellow drivers and their pit crews.

But Lyn was not ready for the rocking chair, knitting needles and herd of cats yet! She published her autobiography, *The Ride of Your Life—A Race Car Driver's Journey* in May 2002, and a year later her

LSJ Foundation hosted the first-ever "Women's in the Winner's Circle" event, where for the first time ever an international gathering of women auto racers convened to address the challenges women encounter in the sport. Her second book, entitled *Oh By the Way...* was released in 2003 as a followup to her earlier autobiography.

St. James is still a force to be reckoned with, yet this time on a different podium. She's a much-in-demand speaker for businesses and philanthropic organizations around the world and has carved out a nice career as a sports commentator for ABC/ESPN as an Indy race analyst and a pit reporter. She was recently nominated for an Ace Award for her on-air work for the Showtime Network.

St. James has made frequent guest appearances on NBC's *The Today Show* and *The David Letterman Show,* ABC's *Good Morning America, the Bob Vila Show,* CNN, Lifetime, Oxygen, PBS, TNN, FOX and Speedvision. And there are few race drivers who can claim that they've been invited to the White House by three sitting Presidents—Ronald Reagan, George Bush and Bill Clinton—but Lyn St. James has been to Washington and has met them all.

Lyn St. James' outstanding career record includes competing in 15 Indy races, including the CART championship and the Indy Racing League, as well scoring two top-10 qualifying spots and one top-10 finish. She holds 31 international and national closed-circuit speed records over a 20-year period and has raced the 12 Hours of Sebring 9 times. She has raced in 53 SCCA Trans-Am races, scoring seven top-five finishes, and in 62 IMSA GT races, notching six wins and 17 top-five and 37 top-10 finishes. She is also the only solo woman racer to have ever won an IMSA GT race.

In 2007, her LSJ Foundation released a "Women in the Winner's Circle" 18-Month Calendar, featuring Melanie Troxel, Danica Patrick, Katherine Legge, Erin Crocker, Sarah Fisher, Jutta Kleinschmidt and other women drivers influenced by St. James over the years. To this day, Lyn continues to serve on numerous boards, including the Indiana Governor's Council for Physical Fitness and Sports (as vice chair), and she is the chair of the Advisory Board of the Colorado Silver Bullets, the first all-female baseball team in the North American Professional Baseball League.

The National Association for Girls and Women in Sport awarded St. James their 2001 Guiding Women in Sports award and was selected by Sports Illustrated as one of the "Top 100 Women Athletes of the Century." *Working Woman* magazine also listed her as one of the "350 Women Who Changed the World Between 1976–1996." She and her husband Roger divide their time between homes in Daytona Beach, Indianapolis and Vail.

Chapter Twelve

Barbara Armstrong

United Kingdom
(1966–)

Although this two-time British Rally Champion sounds more like a character out of an Agatha Christie novel, she is actually one of Britain's most competitive rally drivers. As she is also academically qualified in both garden and interior design, Barbara Armstrong dreams of someday funneling her love of cooking into running a catering business or perhaps even trying her hand at farming.

But dear Miss Marple could never compete with Barbara in the automotive world, where she has become one of the more recognizable figures behind the wheel of her powerful Porsche or Peugeot rally cars. Barbara got her first taste for rallying while working on her father's farm alongside a fellow who owned a rally car. One day she got up the nerve to ask for a chance to co-drive, and fortunately for the sport, he said yes.

Debuting in 1984, Barbara scored her first win in 1989 then started competing regularly in the annual Peugeot Challenge. In 1992, she became a rally instructor at Silverstone Race Circuit, and in 1996, became a works driver for SEAT Sport UK, winning the British Ladies title for them in 1998 and 1999, thanks in great part to Gary Savage, Head of SEAT Cupra Sport.

In 2001, Armstrong thought it was time for a vehicular change and got behind the wheel of a Porsche; however, it was in her favorite Peugeot that she scored an impressive second-overall finish in the World Cup Rally that year. Since 2003, Armstrong has taken on coordinating championship races such as the UK Formula Ford and Volkswagen Racing Cups. She has also become the chief instructor at the SEAT Race School, located at Prodrive's test track near Kenilworth. Ruling the roost like a mother hen, Barbara oversees the track education of 20 young women race and rally drivers, instilling them with her ruthless determination and competitiveness.

She currently holds a number of driving licenses that enable her to compete internationally both in cars and on motorcycles, and she frequently makes guest speaker appearances, recounting her rallying experiences and commenting from the unique perspective of a woman competing in a man's sport.

Armstrong is careful to ensure that she maintains balance in her life, and when not driving hell bent for leather, she collects wooden ducks, enjoys cooking for friends and sharing a good bottle of Chardonnay, loves jet skiing and defies gravity piloting her glider.

To add even more levity to her life, Barbara, along with other UK women rally drivers, shed their race suits and helmets for a 2007 "Gravel Girls" charity calendar to benefit the Wales Air Ambulance service, which saved the life of up-and-coming young rally racer, Nicola Parker, when she suffered a severe head injury after a frightening accident late in 2006. Parker's Subaru Impreza had careened off a gravel track and had become lodged 30 feet down in a steep ravine. Fortunately, both Nicola and her co-driver were rescued from the near-fatal wreck by the Wales Air Ambulance.

Now entering her 40s, Barbara Armstrong still has dreams of winning a big international rally and her indomitable spirit and enthusiasm may just get her on that road.

WOMEN OF THE NEW MILLENIUM

Chapter Thirteen

Sarah Fisher

Columbus, Ohio, United States
(1980–)

Born just outside of Columbus, Ohio, Sarah started off racing in midgets, having spent many a weekend accompanying her parents, Dave and Reba, to the local tracks where her father raced in sprint cars. By age five, the racing bug had caught hold of her so tightly that her parents relented and fitted her out in a quarter-midget, in which she raced, along with go-karts, until she was in her teens. Along the way, she won the 1991, 1993 and 1994 World Karting Association Grand National Championships as well as the Circleville Points Championship in 1993.

By age 15, Sarah was already an old hand at racing Winged Outlaw Sprint cars, having chalked up numerous wins, including the 1995 Dirt Track Racing Round-Up Rookie of the Year. She was very successful in the Outlaw Sprint cars, and by 1997, she was named to the 62-race All Star Circuit of Champions series, where she scored a hard-fought second-place finish at Eldora Speedway.

In 1998, the 5'3" blonde and her dad, who was also her crew chief, sought out new challenges, and soon Sarah was racing in Automobile Racing Club of America (ARCA), North American Auto Racing Series (NAMARS) and United States Auto Club (USAC)-sanctioned events, maintaining a competitive schedule that helped prepare her for her future transition to the Indy Racing League (IRL).

With another successful season under her belt, and after having picked up two track records and five feature wins along the way, the IRL beckoned Sarah to sign on. In 1999, she became the youngest person ever to pass the IRL Rookie Test. She ran her first IRL IndyCar Series event at Texas Motor Speedway later in the year, posting a disappointing 25th-place finish because of a mechanical failure going into lap 66.

The next year, Fisher signed on to drive for Derrick Walker's IRL IndyCar Series team, running eight races in the Indy Racing Northern Light Series; and in May 2000, she entered the history books when she became just the third woman and one of the youngest drivers ever to compete in the Indianapolis 500.

She was also the youngest person ever to lead laps during an IRL IndyCar event at Kentucky Speedway, as well as the youngest woman to take the podium, scoring a third-place finish. Sarah scored more podiums in 2001, starting with a second-place finish at the IRL's inaugural race at Homestead Miami Speedway, which was the best result ever for a woman driver in Indy-style racing.

As the next season approached, Fisher was hired by Dreyer & Reinbold Racing to replace the injured Robbie Buhl in their No. 24 Purex/Aventis car for the IndyCar Series event at Nazareth Speedway. Fisher did not disappoint and came in fourth. Dreyer & Reinbold Racing, suitably impressed with her performance, decided to create a second racing team for the 2002 season with Fisher at the wheel. She responded by becoming the fastest-ever woman qualifier for the Indianapolis 500 in May of that year, averaging a speed of over 229 miles per hour. Although she ran only 10 of the series' 15 races, she still logged a career best finish with an 18th place in the IndyCar Series Championship point standings.

Fisher finished in 21st place at the 2004 Indianapolis 500, this time driving for the Kelly Racing team, but she was distracted, already looking ahead to the bigger, more popular arena of stock car racing. Later that year while attending a function in Washington, D.C., hosted by Chevrolet, she met Richard Childress and started talking about racing in a couple NASCAR series, in particular Busch and Nextel. Childress recognized that familiar fire in the belly and ended up offering Sarah a three-year contract. During her inaugural season, she scored four top-10 finishes, securing a 12th-place finish in the points standing, just outside of the chase for the NASCAR Grand National Division West Series title. It did, however, make her eligible to compete in the 3rd Annual NASCAR Toyota All-Star Showdown at Irwindale Speedway, where she finished a healthy 11th.

In 2005, Fisher entered NASCAR's new Drive for Diversity program behind the wheel of the No.20 Chevrolet Monte Carlo for the Bill McAnally Racing/Richard Childress Racing Development Program. But after a year racing in the big leagues of stock cars, Fisher failed to secure a ride, so she decided to return to IRL in 2006, rejoining the Dreyer & Reinbold Racing team in time for the Kentucky Speedway event, where she started in 12th and finished in 12th in the No.5 Dallara Honda. Then at the Chicagoland Speedway season finale, Fisher again started and finished in the same position, this time in 16th.

It's not all racing for Sarah, though, as she is working towards a bachelor's degree in marketing, taking part-time classes at Ellis College, and she also works part-time for an Atlanta marketing company, Ignition Inc. She also enjoys time at home in Indianapolis with her fiancé, Andy O'Gara, who also works as lead mechanic in the IRL, and with Wrigley, their chocolate Labrador.

To keep herself in top physical shape for racing, Sarah chows down on pasta and protein foods the night before a race and then, just before she suits up, nibbles on fresh strawberries. Superstition also plays a part in her day-to-day living as Sarah makes a conscious effort to ensure that there are always nine goldfish alive and swimming in her fish tank.

Always popular with fans and fellow racers, Sarah has won the Most Popular Driver Award four times and lends her support to a number of charities, especially those involving children. She is also a media darling and has been interviewed on all the major television news and chat shows, including ABC's *Good Morning America*, CBS' *This Morning*, NBC's *Nightly News*, *The Tonight Show with Jay Leno*, *Live with Regis and Kelly* and *Real Sports with Bryant Gumbel*. Her photo has graced the pages of *Sports Illustrated*, *People*, *Teen People*, *Cosmo Girl*, *Seventeen*, *Glamour* and *Mademoiselle*, just to name a few.

Sarah Fisher continues to race with a fiery passion that is sure to keep her on those pages.

Chapter Fourteen

Danica Patrick

Beloit, Wisconsin, United States
(1982–)

What else can be written about Danica Patrick that hasn't already been printed, broadcast, blogged or discussed around water coolers? The gorgeous and talented driver of the Andretti Green Racing No.7 Indy car has been on the cover of nearly every sports magazine, on TV talk shows, has her own website and weekly race blog and has been, as Justin Timberlake would say, "Bringing Sexy Back" to the sport of Indy car racing.

Born March 25, 1982, in Beloit, Wisconsin, Danica Sue Patrick grew up in Roscoe, Illinois, playing Barbie dolls with her sister Brooke. Both her parents were big racing fans: her dad, T.J., used to race snowmobiles, motocross bikes and midget cars, while her mom, Beverly, worked as a mechanic. At age 10, Danica and her sister were offered go-karting lessons, and as soon as Danica got behind the wheel, she fell in love with the idea of whizzing around the track. Brooke quickly tired of karting, but not Danica, who joined the World Karting Association (WKA) and started on her road to glory racing at the Sugar River Raceway outside of Brodhead, Wisconsin.

T.J. and Beverley Patrick spent their summer weekends taxiing their young daughter to tracks across the state, and within two years, Danica had become a force to be reckoned with on the track. She captured the WKA Grand National Championship in 1994 in the Yamaha Sportsman class, and she followed that up with additional karting titles in both 1995 and 1996. She finished out her final season in the WKA in 1997 by winning the Grand National Championship in the Yamaha Lite and HPV classes, then made a big decision. It was time to move on, this time all the way across the Atlantic to England where she could better upgrade her skills; she joined the Formula Vauxhall Winter Series.

Danica competed in a reduced racing schedule in the UK throughout 1998, due mainly to the fact that she was busy honing her driving skills at the Formula Ford racing school in Canada. It wasn't until 1999 that she made her actual British racing debut, finishing her first full season with a respectable ninth-place standing. Next year,

Danica improved her points standing and moved all the way up to second place at the Formula Ford Festival; this also marked the best-ever finish by an American at the British event.

Danica left England at the end of 2001, but still managed to make headlines back in the U.S. when she was awarded the Gorsline Scholarship Award for Top Upcoming Road Racing Driver. She also competed in the tough British Zetek Formula Ford Championship, after which Danica was named the top female open-wheel driver with international experience.

In 2002, she attracted the attention of the scouts from Team Rahal Letterman of the Indy Racing League. After signing a multi-year contract with Rahal Letterman, Danica then spent two years toiling in the lower ranks, working on her sense of speed and timing as well as learning race strategies and the politics of the circuit. She made several starts in the Barber Dodge pro Series before moving over to the Toyota Atlantic Series in 2003. As soon as Danica scored her first pole position and podium result in that series, the first for any female driver, the management at Rahal Letterman Racing decided to move her up to IndyCar. She paid them back with an impressive third-place finish in the 2004 Atlantic Championship point standings. Danica Patrick was now on the road to the big leagues.

Danica became Rahal Letterman Racing's third driver for the 2005 Indy season, and she made her debut at the 2005 Toyota Indy 300, where she raced hard but was knocked out on lap 158. Many considered her to be a young racing prodigy as she raced throughout her rookie year, and her skills were never better showcased than in the series' biggest race, the Indianapolis 500.

She was only the fourth woman ever to compete in the legendary race—following Janet Guthrie, Lyn St. James and Sarah Fisher—and as the date drew near, the media hype surrounding her participation grew and spun out of control. As the public's new darling, Danica lived and practiced during the weeks leading up to the event under constant media scrutiny.

Exhibiting maturity far beyond her years, Danica acquitted herself well on the track despite all the pressure and led a total of 19 laps before being forced back into the pack. As the race drew to a close, she drove back hard to the front and finished in fourth, a women's record, thereby dispelling any doubt about her ability to compete with the big boys. Danica Patrick had proven that she belonged.

But her success did not come without some controversy, and she has definitely paid the price for mixing it up in the boys' sandbox. For example, other racers on the Indy circuit and even some motor sport journalists have complained that her light bodyweight—Danica weighs in at around 100 lbs and stands barely 5'2"—gives her an unfair advantage by making her car considerably lighter and faster in a sport that requires strict regulation of engine size and car weight. IRL officials were quick to reassure all her competitors that Danica's weight had no effect on her racing prowess; and to prove she was no "light-weight," she finished 12th in the 2005 IndyCar Series championship with a total of 325 points.

As the most successful woman driver on the Indy circuit, she has also had to deal with anti-quated attitudes and sexist remarks from old-school macho racers who still feel that auto racing is a man's sport; yet Danica's determination and toughness shines through all the adversity. She was even more focused in 2006, as if she was out to prove all the naysayers wrong: she was not just a "pretty face in a big fast car." She went on the offensive in the media and made numerous appearances on TV talk shows like *Late Night with David Letterman,* who just happens to be one of her bosses. She also teamed up with legendary NASCAR racer Rusty Wallace to drive the Rolex 24 at Daytona and qualified again for the Indianapolis 500.

But the 2006 race season started on a sad note, with a horrific crash at the Toyota Indy 300, held at Homestead Miami Speedway. Patrick qualified third, but in the final practice sessions on the morning of the race, her Rahal Letterman Racing teammate, Paul Dana, was killed in a vicious accident. Captured on camera, Dana's car had stalled around the blind side of a corner and was smashed from behind by another driver going full bore around the corner. Danica and fellow Rahal Letterman driver Buddy Rice immediately withdrew from the race as a show of solidarity for their fallen teammate.

Danica resumed her 2006 IRL campaign in the following race at St. Petersburg, Florida, where she finished sixth. She followed that with an eighth-place finish in Japan, an eighth at the Watkins Glen race, and at the Indy 500, she again finished in eighth after having started in 10th on the grid. The following week, the team switched over to the Dallara chassis, a move that almost proved disastrous. The team couldn't seem to get the new car up to race level, and Danica struggled to remain competitive. She managed to score fourth-place finishes in both Nashville and Milwaukee, which helped her advance to ninth in the overall point standings. But bad luck returned at Michigan, where her car died in the final laps of the race. She had her mojo back by the end of the season and recorded a ninth-place finish in the season's point standings, moving up three places from her rookie year.

As the 2006 season drew to a close, she announced that she had signed on with the Andretti Green Racing team and would campaign in the No.7 Dallara Honda in 2007, replacing their previous driver, Bryan Herta.

The 2007 season, though, did not go well for Danica. Although she had the support and enthusiasm of a new team, it seemed as if Lady Luck was not on her side. At Homestead-Miami Speedway in March, she finished a disappointing 14th after crashing and being forced out of the race. She then finished in eighth place at St. Petersburg, followed by a dismal 11th in Japan. She managed a little better in Kansas and placed seventh, but at the Indy 500 she had more bad luck when rain forced a finish under caution just as she was working her way back up through the pack. Danica was also plagued by accidents throughout the first half of the 2007 season; but again, her steely determination helped her through the spell bad luck and loss of point standings.

One bright light came in April 2007 when she launched her official fan club and website. The thousands of "Danica Maniacs," as her fans are known, helped boost her morale during the dark hours and poor finishes, posting message after message of encouragement and well-wishing on the discussion boards. She also had the love and support of her husband, Paul Edward Hospenthal, and her miniature schnauzer, Billy, at their home in Phoenix, Arizona.

Her father, T.J., is easily her most devoted fan, driving his daughter's motor home to each event as well as managing her website. He and mother Bev take care of the official Danica Patrick merchandise that fans gobble up at each of her track appearances. The little down time Danica does manage to squeeze out of her schedule is spent weight training, running and doing yoga. She loves listening to artists like Alanis Morissette, Nelly, Norah Jones and Queen, and she enjoys the wacky comedy films of Adam Sandler, Will Ferrell and Jim Carrey, as well as the old black and white westerns of the '40s and '50s.

Her website gives an insightful piece of advice, which is probably appropriate for every fast lady listed in this book: "Drive like you have something to prove every time...." Danica Patrick continues to prove that she can drive just as fast and hard as any man out there.

Chapter Fifteen

Erin Crocker

Wilbraham, Massachusetts, United States
(1981–)

Growing up in Wilbraham, Massachusetts, Erin was the youngest of five children. While she was still a toddler, Erin's father introduced the family to racing, and as she watched her older brothers speed around the tracks, she would fidget and fuss, wanting to take the wheel herself.

At the age of seven, Erin got her chance and started racing competitively in Custom Quarter Midgets for a club out of Thompson, Connecticut, and the Silver City Quarter Midget Club out of Meriden, Connecticut. In the following nine years, she amassed countless regional and national titles, including Female Driver of the Year in 1993, 1994 and 1995, as well as North East Regional Champion from 1993 to 1996. By the age of 16, she had set her sights firmly on a full-time career behind the wheel.

She skillfully balanced her racing demands with high school participating in several varsity sports, such as soccer, tennis, lacrosse and skiing. She also became vice president of her class and was a National Honor Society affiliate. She eventually went on to attend the Rensselaer Polytechnic Institute in Troy, New York, where she graduated in 2003 with a Bachelor of Industrial and Management Engineering.

During her sophomore year in 1997, Erin could be found racing at Whip City Speedway in Westfield, Massachusetts, behind the wheel of a 600cc micro sprint, earning her Rookie of the Year accolades; she also became the youngest driver and first female to win a feature race there. The following year, she competed at the same track in a 1200cc Mini sprint, driving for the Central New York Mini Sprint Association (CNYMS).

She competed in the Eastern Limited Sprint (ELS) series throughout 1999 and was again honored with the Rookie of the Year title. Over the next two years, Erin raced a few sprint car races with the Empire Super Sprints (ESS), and in 2000, she was given the opportunity to drive a PRO truck with the former PRO Tour Truck series.

Towards the end of 2001, eight-time ESS champion Mike Wooding took notice of her talent and tenacity and asked Erin to drive a 360 winged sprint car for him. After finishing up the 2002 season with five feature wins and 12 heat events, Erin earned the Outstanding Newcomer Award from the National Sprint Car Hall of Fame and was subsequently bombarded with national media attention.

The attention enabled her to secure a unique sponsor: her school, the Rensselaer Polytechnic Institute. At the time, the school was campaigning to promote interest in the institute as well as providing support for spearheading women making strides in male-dominated environments, such as engineering and auto racing. The following season, Erin competed in the USAC Silver Crown Series before switching to 410 Dirt Sprints, becoming the first woman to qualify for the Knoxville Nationals and again winning Rookie of the Year honors. Woodring Racing had her competing in the full 2004 season of the highly competitive World of Outlaws Series, where she won her feature event at Tulare, California.

Then in 2005, Erin Crocker found a new mentor in Ray Evernham. The former crew chief for Winston Cup (now Nextel) champion Jeff Gordon and owner of Evernham Motorsports brought Erin into his development program (the first woman to participate), where she was soon competing in the ARCA RE/MAX Series, NASCAR Busch Series and

NASCAR Truck Series. Making her truck series debut at Phoenix International Raceway in November 2005, she competed at the season finale at Homestead-Miami Speedway and also made four NASCAR Busch Series starts at Richmond, Dover, Memphis and Phoenix, with her best finish of 29th coming at Memphis. Crocker also ran a six-race ARCA schedule in 2005, scoring four top-fives and five top-10 finishes and two poles.

Crocker stepped up for Evernham Motorsports in 2006 and then put her foot down hard on the gas, launching her NASCAR Truck Series driving the No.98 Cheerios/Betty Crocker Dodge Ram. She made her Busch series debut in September that same year at Richmond International Raceway and also managed to squeeze in a few ARCA and USAC Silver Crown Series races.

Looking ahead to the 2007 season, Erin is set to compete in the NASCAR Busch Series with team-mates Kasey Kahne, Elliott Sadler, Boris Said and Scott Riggs, driving the No.9 Dodge Charger for Evernham. She continues to hone her skills behind the wheel to meet her longterm goals, which include driving in the Indy 500, racing's Holy Grail, as well as full-time racing in Nextel Cup or IRL.

Apart from having great natural talent in a race car, Erin is athletic and stays in great physical condition. She possesses the determination and the commitment to overcome all obstacles, especially those unexpected glitches that come from living in the public eye. Her rumored romantic relationship with Ray Evernham has created some dissention in the team's ranks, although both she and Ray have ably dodged any blatant questions from the racing press about it. Erin also takes great pleasure in the pre-race meet and greets with her fans and has quickly acquired a considerable amount of media savvy.

Often referred to as "NASCAR's answer to Danica Patrick," Erin takes the ribbing well and is encouraged by all the attention showered on the female drivers. She has said that all the interviews and magazine covers have had a positive effect on securing sponsors, who are now more willing to consider sticking their logos on cars driven by females, and as a result it has become easier for women to secure good equipment and better crews.

Luckily for her, Erin's mother owns some really "good equipment"—an inherited '57 Corvette that Erin hopes to own herself one day—but in the meantime, her favorite off-track vehicle is the Dodge Viper. And, as far as driving as a civilian on public roads, Erin often finds herself losing patience with the slowpokes, especially those who just crawl along in the left lane, and most of all she hates sudden lane jumpers. So watch out, Tony Stewart, and keep an eye on your rear bumper; Ms. Crocker is well on her way.

Chapter Sixteen

Katherine Legge

Guilford, Surrey, United Kingdom

(1980–)

Katherine Legge is one cool customer on the track. Not only is she considered a real "hottie" by her legions of male race fans, but she's also one of the gutsiest racers in Champ Car, having survived a horrific crash in September of 2006 before getting right back behind the wheel less than a week later for a one-day test session.

The attractive Brit was born in 1980 in Guilford, Surrey, and it wasn't long before her father, Derek, realized his little girl was going to live her life in the fast lane. Katherine always wanted daddy to go faster anytime she was in the car, so while mum, Vivienne, was away on a trip, Dad secretly invested in a go-kart and crash helmet for his little speedster. By the time her mother returned, there was no way Katherine would ever give up her kart; she was practically glued to the seat every waking moment.

So while Katherine got her wish for wheels granted, there was a catch: she had to maintain good grades at school. To help her achieve academic success, her parents enrolled her in an all-girls school, effectively removing unnecessary distractions such as boys; and it worked. Katherine completed her education with an exemplary record of eight General Certificates of Secondary Education (GCSEs) and four A-Levels.

Between 1990 and 1998, Katherine competed in numerous British karting championships and established herself as a winning driver, attracting interest from the racing community. She also found herself racing alongside future Formula One

Katherine Legge on the track at the 2007 Toronto Grand Prix

stars like Jenson Button, Anthony Davidson and current wünderkind, Lewis Hamilton.

As the millennium drew to a close, her hobby became a profession and in 2000, Legge started racing in the British Formula Ford Zetec Championship. Her best finish was third place and she became the first female to win a pole position in the series.

In 2001, she moved into the British Formula Renault Winter Series and the following year, Legge claimed the pole position at Oulton Park with a time that trounced Kimi Raikkonen's lap record. In 2002, Legge became the first woman to be honored as one of the British Racing Drivers' Club Rising Stars, and to commemorate her recording the fastest lap speed by a female in the U.K., she was presented with the Susan TP Jamieson Award.

She spent 2003 honing her driving skills, racing in select rounds of the British Formula 3 Championship. Then in 2004, Legge competed in both the British Formula Renault and North American Formula Renault Can-Am Cup, finishing 10th in the North American series point standings even though she started in less than half of the scheduled race events. This commendable performance earned her the Kathryn Nunn Infinity Pro Series Scholarship.

Following such a stellar year, Legge worked even harder in the off-season, successfully testing for the Polestar Racing Group and impressing all who saw her on the track. Champ Car World Series and PKV Racing co-owner Kevin Kalkhoven was one of those she impressed, and he enthusiastically agreed to sponsor her in the upcoming 2005 Atlantic series.

Enjoying her first full season as a professional racer, Katherine blew away the competition in the 2005 Toyota Atlantic series and scored three wins, the first coming in her spectacular debut race at Long Beach, followed by back-to-back wins at Edmonton and San Jose. The Long Beach victory was the first win recorded by a woman in a major North American open-wheel race, and this achievement later earned Legge Southern California's Top Racing Moment of 2005 Award, as voted by race fans. She logged further podiums with a third-place finish at Portland and a second place at the Road America event. Katherine ended her rookie season with a third-place finish in the Atlantic Championship standings and was voted *RACER* magazine's Most Promising Road Racer by fans around the world. And just as her dad was adding another shelf to the trophy case, she won the 2005 Atlantic Championship Series BBS Rising Star Award.

Katherine made the record books during the off-season by becoming the first woman in over a decade to have an official Formula One test.

Behind the wheel of a Minardi F1 car, she posted the second-fastest time among five drivers who tested for the team in Italy. She also tested for Great Britain's A1 Grand Prix Team and drove a Champ Car for Rocketsports Racing for the first time at Sebring.

Legge was instantly taken with Champ Car, and in February 2006, PKV Racing announced that Katherine Legge would join the team for the 2006 Champ Car season. Less than four months later, she became the first woman to lead a lap in the history of the series, and with a sixth-place finish at Milwaukee, an eighth at Cleveland and a ninth at Denver, Legge was poised to challenge for Rookie of the Year honors as well as helping drive England towards a potential championship in the Nations Cup. But in September, everything came to a screeching halt when Katherine was involved in a horrendous accident.

During the closing stages of the Road America race at Elkhart Lake, the rear wing of her car inexplicably broke off, causing Legge to lose control of the aerodynamically unstable car. She barrel-rolled across the track and slammed into the catch fence, her car shattering into pieces while miraculously leaving the cockpit intact. With the flames raging all around her, Katherine managed to regain her composure, and as the emergency rescue crew arrived, she was already trying to claw her way out of the wreckage. Unbelievably, she walked away from the smoldering ruin that had been her car.

Katherine was left with only some bruising to her knees and a new appreciation for the strength and durability of the big Champ Cars. Five days later, Katherine was back on board her PKV Racing Lola, running a one-day test at Sebring International Raceway. She ran 150 miles on the 1.66-mile course, logging a best lap time of 51.8 seconds. In an interview given shortly afterwards, Legge stated, "As soon as I drove out of pit lane for the first run, I felt like I always have. I had no issues getting back in the car— it actually felt good."

Legge earned her racing stripes that day, along with the respect of her fellow drivers. She was eventually forced out of the Surfer's Paradise race in Australia at the end of October and had to watch the checkered flag drop from pit row; but she was back into competition mode in November's Mexico GP, where she scored a 16th-place finish. The Mexico race, however, resulted in further injuries when Legge was hit by Mario Dominguez, and she found herself back in the infield medical facilities, where X-rays showed a broken thumb. Two metal screws later, she wrapped her hand back around a steering wheel and was back on the throttle shortly afterwards.

The Dale Coyne Racing team came knocking at the beginning of the 2007 season, and Katherine happily signed on with them for the upcoming campaign. Her new teammate, Bruno Junqueira, also brought a new inspiration to Katherine's driving strategy. Feeling that Bruno had a similar driving style to her own, she said, "Perhaps I can learn a little bit from him. He's placed second on numerous occasions and maintained regular top-10 finishes. If I can catch up and pass him, then I know I'm on track for victory..."

Legge ran the Daytona 24-Hours event with George Robinson and Paul and Wally Dallenbach as co-drivers in the No.84 Daytona Prototype, a bigger, slower car than she was used to in the Champ Car models, but "still a lot of fun to drive" according to Katherine. She now aims to compete in the legendary Le Mans 24-Hours and the Indy 500.

Although there is a lot of emphasis placed on a driver's strength and endurance inside the car, Katherine has a simple physical fitness regime to build herself up physically, mentally and emotionally for the rigors of racing: a bit of weight training and gym workouts throughout the week coupled with a healthy diet is all it takes for her to be on top of her game. "Sure I run the course through my mind prior to each race, but driving isn't an issue any more," she states confidently, "but no matter how clean a race may be, my mum still doesn't like to watch. The Toronto Grand Prix was the first race in years that she's actually attended."

Katherine gets to see her family frequently, maintaining homes in both Northamptonshire, England, and in Indianapolis. When she's not racing, she indulges in her other favorite hobbies of mountain biking, skiing and swimming. And with such a busy, active lifestyle, it's not surprising that her favorite food is energy-packed pasta. She is also supportive and encouraging of other young women coming into auto racing; however, she doesn't expect any special treatment based on her gender: "I don't consider myself a 'woman' auto racer, I am an auto racer...period," Legge adamantly states. "Sure, it's difficult trying to get the good equipment, the sponsorship and the respect of the fans and media, but that's what every driver encounters, so I just concentrate on the driving and proving that I belong by simply doing my best."

Like most young drivers, Katherine's ultimate goal is Formula One, but that is still a way off. It's not all glamour and luxury being a professional race-car driver: one needs sponsors to underwrite the millions of dollars it takes to run a single team each year, crews to man the pits, and now more than ever, media skills. But Katherine has proved that she is a real pro when it comes to interviews, and she knows how to intrigue and humor reporters.

On qualifying day at the 2007 Toronto GP, Katherine challenged teammate Bruno to a "sumo wrestling" match in a temporary ring constructed in "thunder alley" for the race fans. It was a best-out-of-three rounds match, and in front of her cheering pit crew and hundreds of spectators,

Katherine Legge in her sumo-wrestling suit at the 2007 Toronto Grand Prix

Katherine charged across the ring at Bruno, bouncing her inflated plastic sumo suit off his. Both refused to drop until Katherine slipped, and she tumbled to the ground. Bruno plopped down on top of her, pinning her for a 10-count. She was laughing so much the second time that she didn't see Bruno charging again and he took her down easily, both laughing hysterically. The crowd went wild, mum and dad Legge clapped enthusiastically and the Dale Coyne race team cheered for their drivers. For a few moments, the tension and anticipation of the next day's race seemed to disappear.

This is what Katherine Legge is all about—for her, racing must be fun and everywhere she competes she exudes a sense of mischief and of humor. Although the 2007 season was not the most successful, her positive approach to the sport keeps her in good stead for whatever the year might bring.

Chapter Seventeen

Ashley Taws

Toronto, Ontario, Canada

(1983–)

In the testosterone-charged arena of stock car racing, the sight of a bright pink "Barbie at Wal-Mart Be Anything U Can Be" BMW gets everyone's attention. And little Barbie-playing girls with big dreams of checkered flags and fast cars have a brilliant role model in 23-year-old Canadian racer, Ashley Taws.

Ashley began racing in earnest in 2000, and the pretty teenager soon became a Canadian fan favorite. They lined the racetracks and cheered her fearlessness and strategy that far exceeded her years and racing experience. But towards the end of 2002, a dreadful highway crash threatened her career and her life. Only Ashley's steely determination and months of intense therapy got her back into racing again, but within months the seemingly invincible young driver was once more reunited with her car, the "Barbie Beamer."

But before we reach that happy ending we should go back to Ashley's own starting grid, back to when she was 10 years old and her dad, Peter, bought a go-kart for her brother, Doug. At that time, Ashley, like most little girls, was far too busy playing with her Barbie doll collection to pay any mind to the dirt and grime of karting. Peter, busy with his son's racing schedule, always invited Ashley along when he took Doug to the various racetracks around Ontario. On one such trip, he encouraged Ashley to give it a try, and to everyone's surprise, the little girl was a natural.

Each weekend, the family went racing at the Toronto Kart Club (TKC), and Ashley and Doug took turns manning the kart. Despite competing in only half of the races that first season, Ashley placed an impressive seventh in the club's championship standings.

Peter, realizing that he had a unique talent on his hands, bought Ashley her own go-kart. The next season, Ashley raced a full calendar of events and finished second in the Novice Division, only behind the racetrack owner's son. Not too shabby for a young girl who only a year ago was too busy playing with her Barbie dolls to think about racing against silly boys!

Her brother gradually lost interest in karts, but by the mid-'90s, Ashley had already become a fierce competitor and a fan favorite at TKC among other places across Ontario. She was awarded Rookie of the Year honors in 1996 at the TKC's Junior Championship, where she finished out the season in second place, and then she hit the podium again later that year in the Ontario Trillium Series, logging a third-place finish. By the end of the year, she had claimed the Canadian Grand National Championship honors and was setting her sights on a professional racing career.

By 1998, Ashley was ready for something faster than the four-cycle go-karts she had been driving, so Peter arranged for her to change to two-cycle motors, which produced far greater power and speed. The change was more than successful, and by the end of the season, the Taws family trophy case was literally full to overflowing with Ashley's trophies, including a second straight Canadian Grand National Cup, a win in the Formula 100 Junior Division and a second-place finish in the regional Formula 100 Junior championship standings.

The following season, Ashley spent a great deal of time researching her racing options while maintaining a limited karting schedule, and in 2000, she finally made the move into Formula 1200 cars. She proceeded to impress all who witnessed her rookie year with five top-three finishes, including two wins behind the wheel of her Maximum Benefit/Big Sisters auto. She placed third in the Isseco/ Kumho Formula 1200 Championship, second in the CASC-OR (Canadian Automobile Sport Clubs—Ontario Region) Race Ontario Sprints and second in the BARC (British Automobile Racing Club) Formula 1200 Championship. And as if that wasn't enough, she capped off her first season in Formula 1200 with the BARC Bob Attrell Award for Best New Driver and the Muriel B. Knap Trophy for Sportsmanship, Ability and Sparkle.

In 2001, two of the world's most recognized brand names came calling. Mattel's premiere brand, Barbie, joined with one of North America's biggest chain stores, Wal-Mart, financed a sponsorship agreement and created the pink and purple "Be Anything with Barbie at Wal-Mart" Ford race car, destined to be driven by Ashley.

At first the car with the "girly" paint scheme was the object of derision; Ashley's track mates joked about her "Barbie-mobile" or her "Malibu Camper." But, as the girl kept winning, suddenly the Barbie car wasn't funny any more: Ashley was becoming a force to be reckoned with.

Throughout the season, Taws and the pink car led the pack in just about every race. The competition was so fierce that the championship came down to the final race of the season. Again, Ashley was the "bridesmaid," ultimately finishing second in the final standings. Still impressing people, she was awarded the Muriel B. Knap Trophy for the second year in a row.

Ashley spent the next two years honing her driving skills in Formula 1200 before she got "the itch." With her key sponsors secured, Taws embarked upon her debut Canadian Formula Ford Championship campaign in 2002. Her "Be Anything with Barbie at Wal-Mart" Ford was the undisputed crowd favorite throughout the Formula 1600 series, and she spent hours signing autographs and meeting fans at each of the big-ticket events. On the track, she was setting records for female racers by becoming the first woman in the history of the series to stand on the podium after both a third-place finish at the start of the season and a second-place finish later that year.

One of her most exciting races was at the Toronto Indy. She had successfully qualified to take the pole position on the starting grid; however, due to a series of mechanical problems, she was forced to the back of the pack. During the race, the crowd slowly rose to its feet and started cheering as the Barbie car fought its way back, lap after lap, until Ashley had bullied her way to a fourth-place finish, almost nudging out the third-place car at the finish line.

The excitement of the 2002 racing season had everyone in the Taws family hopeful for a great sophomore year in Formula 1600. However, as the

Ashley Taws with her "Barbie at Wal-Mart Be Anything U Can Be" Super Touring BMW

Christmas decorations went up and letters to Santa were mailed, Ashley's future prospects all but disappeared in a split second. She was riding in the rear passenger seat of a friend's car when the vehicle was struck head-on. Ashley suffered severe internal injuries, including aortic artery damage to her leg and a fractured vertebra in her lower back. It wasn't a matter of whether she would ever drive again, but if she would ever walk.

Before the accident, Ashley had always made a point of visiting the gym regularly and sticking to a strict weight-training program, focusing on upper body strength and abdominals. "Being in such great physical condition was a real benefit to my overall recovery," Taws later stated, "and after going through all those months of surgeries and physiotherapy sessions, I think I amazed the doctors that I was fit and healthy enough to qualify for my division during the 2003 Toronto Indy weekend in July." She was still a little tentative about getting in and out of the car, but there was no denying her hunger for victory as she practically drag raced the top three cars all the way to the finish line, securing a respectable fourth-place finish in her famous pink chariot.

Two weeks later and a lot more confident in the driver's seat, Ashley nailed a third-place finish at the Grand Prix de Trois-Rivières; however, her injuries took a toll on her overall energy and she suffered from fatigue throughout the race. She was forced out of the car once again when a series of abdominal problems landed her back in hospital for further surgery. To this day, she still experiences pain in her back and soreness in her left knee, although by the end of the 2006 racing season, her health and stamina had returned and planning began for the 2007 campaign.

She tested herself by entering the 2007 CASC-OR Ice Racing Series, which runs during the cold winter months. The magic was still there, and she won in the Long Wheelbase Street Stud Class with Jordan Marrison and Brock Gilboe of Vertex Fabworx in attendance. What they saw was a true champion deserving of a position worthy of her talents, so within only a few weeks, they had not only offered her a ride in their Super Touring BMW but struck a deal which included having Barbie back on board with Mattel brand-mate Polly Pockets, Dare Bear Paws, Keystone Benefits Inc. and Kwik Kopy, all of whom saw the potential for greatness in this four-wheeled Cinderella story.

In 2007, Ashley raced both a stock car and the "Barbie at Wal-Mart Be Anything U Can Be" Super Touring BMW, sharing driving duties with Jordan and Brock as she competed in the Ontario Sportsman Series. She also made more than 30 personal appearances at various Wal-Mart locations across North America to meet her fans and to inspire all those other little girls who may be busy tinkering with their Barbie Malibu Campers. "I'm thrilled when other female racers, especially the new girls coming into the sport, tell me that I helped influence their decision to race," Ashley beamed during a trackside interview at 2007's Toronto Steelback Grand Prix. "And I love meeting all the kids who attend the races with their dad, just because the pink Barbie car is on the track."

But Taws can't pay too much attention to all the adoration coming from the grandstands since she's too busy focusing on each corner during the race: "I try to block out everything except the course itself. I pick out my turning and banking spots. And I'm always looking ahead to each corner's entrance and exit points."

This is something she learned early on in her career from both her fellow drivers and from a number of driving coaches, including Jeff Bye who taught her the skills necessary for open-road courses. She was also lucky enough to connect with Keith and Ian Willis of Aim Motor Sports under whose mentorship she forged a successful 2007 campaign in the Barbie BMW.

Although her favorite color may be blue, there's no doubt that we'll soon be seeing a lot more pink at racetracks across the country as Ashley Taws continues to take Barbie out of the playroom and onto the winner's podium.

Chapter Eighteen

Alison MacLeod

Mississauga, Ontario, Canada

(1989–)

How's this for a racing career kick start? Before she was born, Alison MacLeod's father had wanted to name her after legendary NASCAR 'bama gang legend Bobby Allison. Once dad agreed to drop one of the l's, her mother conceded, and so the fate of this future auto racer was sealed; it's been a fast track ever since.

Hailing from Mississauga, a city just west of Toronto, Ontario, young Alison began kart racing at age seven with the support and guidance of her enthusiastic father. On her first attempt to race, Alison crashed out; but she kept at it, and over the next several years, she acquired a passion for the sport and learned a great deal about the mechanics behind kart racing, such as chassis construction and suspension setup.

Her on-track skills proved she was becoming one of the most talented young drivers of recent memory, and in 2002, she was rewarded with the Waterloo Karting Club's championship crown, the first for any female driver. Over the next two seasons, Alison won the 80cc shifter championship at the Mosport Kart Club in 2003 and came in fourth at the 2004 World Karting Association's Winter Nationals in Florida.

At age 13, Alison was nominated for Ford Racing's Female Driver Development Program, and she headed off to attend Bryan Herta's XPlex kart track in Las Vegas for evaluation, where she had to analyze "blind changes" made to her kart. She stunned officials with her innate "feel" for the wheel as she was able to identify all of the alterations made. And after only 24 hours driving on the new track, Alison got to within 0.1 seconds of the local star's record lap time.

The following year, upon recommendation by former Formula One Champ Car driver and Indy Racing League (IRL) team owner Bobby Rahal, she attended a Ford evaluation along with several older female drivers. There, too, Alison was tested for mental acuity, physical strength and on-track ability, along with the all-important media relations. Alison scored high; she tied for first with Erin Crocker, who was eight years her senior and is now an established racer on the NASCAR Craftsman Truck circuit.

By the end of 2004, Alison had also completed the famed Lyn St. James Driver Development Program and realized it was time to put her skills to use. With her dad's support and blessing, Alison tried out for the Ford Focus series, where the cars resembled dune buggies with slicker tires. These "dune buggies," however, were powered by a spec 2.0-litre Ford Focus engine that produced about 170 horsepower.

By age 16, she had secured a 2005 Ford Focus midget ride with legendary midget builder Bob East in Indianapolis and stunned everyone with a fifth-place finish in her first race, a third in her second race and finally winning outright in only her third race. In her fifth race, she placed third behind Stephanie Mockler and Erica Santos, delivering the first-ever all-female U.S. Auto Club (USAC) podium in history.

Alison's on-track successes started coming fast and furious as she became the first-ever Canadian woman to win a USAC race when she won a 50-lap event at the Indianapolis Speedrome in July 2005, and she ended her rookie year in seventh place in the point standings. Later that year, she also competed in other Ford Focus events in Virginia, California and Florida, starting five times in the Kenyon Midget Car Series and scoring two top-10 finishes.

Throughout 2006, MacLeod notched up more great finishes to secure eighth place in Indiana Ford Focus Midget Car Series standings, having competed in 10 of the 13 features and racking up one victory at the Mt. Lawn Speedway in New Castle, Indiana, with a total of six top-10 finishes. She also finished fifth in the Midwest Ford Focus Dirt Midget Car Series.

Alison was not only good on dirt tracks, but she was a great competitor on hard surfaces. She drove in five Midwest Ford Focus Pavement Midget Car Series events, scoring two third-place finishes and a 14th-place finish overall. And if that wasn't enough, she ended the year by winning the Canadian Go-Karting Grand Nationals.

Her driving coach, Bob East, considers MacLeod a natural racing talent and he should know: he has helped several top NASCAR drivers start out their careers, including series champions Jeff Gordon and Tony Stewart. Alison also has a fan in fellow Canadian and champion road racer, Ron Fellows, from whose Karting Championship series she graduated. Both he and East see a clear path for Alison from Midgets to the king of all U.S. auto racing—NASCAR's Nextel series.

But even with all her early success, Alison is most proud of the close relationship she has established with her father. They make weekly 14- to 18-hour round trips together from her Mississauga family home to the various U.S. racetracks where she competes. She shares her dad with her three sisters—Natasha, Sonya and Casey—all of whom are Alison's fans.

Alison's racing heroes include the late Dale Earnhardt and NASCAR's current hot young gun, Carl Edwards, and it goes without saying that there is also a soft spot in her heart for namesake, Bobby Allison. When not racing, Alison can be found playing team games such as volleyball, soccer or basketball with friends and neighbors, as well as enjoying a strenuous bike ride.

As NASCAR prepares to expand its Canadian racing properties, this attractive young Mississauga driver could be one of the country's hottest new stars and a dedicated role model for fast ladies everywhere.

Chapter Nineteen

Ashley Force

Bell Gardens, California, United States

(1982–)

Most racing fans will recognize this famous family name thanks to A&E Network's *Driving Force* reality TV show, which featured drag racing star John Force and his three racing daughters, Ashley, Brittany and Courtney.

Family patriarch John Force is a 13-time NHRA Funny Car champion, a world record holder for the quarter-mile in time (4.665 seconds) and in speed (333.58 miles per hour). He was the only drag racer to have won over 100 NHRA tour events (119), and in 1996, he was named American Motor Racing's Driver of the Year.

Force had always wanted a son to follow him into the family business, but his wife Laurie kept delivering daughters, so setting aside his machismo attitude, he began schooling his girls in the art of drag racing. Ashley was his best student.

For her 16th birthday, John enrolled Ashley in Frank Hawley's Drag Racing School, after which she took up auto shop and welding courses as part of her elective curriculum in high school. She began racing right after graduation, but her mother insisted she complete her college education before embarking on a full-time career behind the wheel. So for three and a half years, Ashley hit the books during the week and on weekends she hit the gas. The former high school cheerleader studied television and film at California State University, Fullerton, graduating with a degree in communications. She has been able to use much of her education to help the Force family's other endeavors, which include *Force TV* where Ashley reports from trackside.

She made dad proud in her rookie season, becoming the third woman ever to win the Mac Tools U.S. Nationals at Indianapolis behind the wheel of her Darien & Meadows dragster. The race is one of drag racing's most prestigious and oldest single events. Ashley scored two more national wins, and at season's end, she and John became the first father/daughter team to win at the NHRA Auto Club Finals at Pomona, California. She was also named NHRA's Rookie of the Year and was Driver of the Year across the Texas, Oklahoma, Louisiana, Mississippi and Tennessee region.

As the 2007 season dawned, John Force announced that for the upcoming campaign, Ashley would move up in classification and would drive a fourth Ford Mustang Funny Car for John Force Racing Inc., Castrol and the Automobile Club of Southern California. In preparation, Ashley spent most of 2006 undergoing supervised testing behind the wheel of a 7000 horsepower drag racing machine, and at 24, Ashley is now almost the same age as her father was when he began his Funny Car career.

Ashley is teamed with first-time crew chief Dean "Guido" Antonelli, who was a 12-year member of the crew that helped her dad win 10 of his 14 NHRA world championships. With a great car, a seasoned crew and a pile of motivated sponsors, which include Castrol GTX, Ford, Auto Club, Brand Source, Mac Tools and Mach 1 Air Services, Ashley is well set to compete against the more seasoned established stars of the NHRA and she is being projected as a serious 2007 Rookie of the Year candidate. Ashley's professional debut was at the opening race of the CARQUEST Auto Parts NHRA Winternationals, which takes place at the Auto Club Raceway in Pomona, California.

John Force's mood may have been just a little on the tense side in the last week of April 2007 when Ashley beat her father fair and square in the first round at the Atlanta Dragway during the NHRA POWERade series. She then went on to beat 2003 champion Tony Pedregon in the second round, hopefully putting a smile back on John's face and giving the team a big boost.

Ashley, only the 10th woman ever licensed to drive a Funny Car, is revving up her hopes of becoming the seventh woman to qualify for an NHRA national event, the first to reach a final round and, ideally, the first to win a race. To keep perspective on her life and to maintain balance between her career and her private time, Ashley admits to being a complete movie junkie, going out to cinemas at least once a week. Her dad is an even bigger Hollywood fanatic, sometimes watching two or three movies a day. Ashley has also tried her hand at producing films, creating video spoofs of classic movies for the team's Christmas parties. One of her films was entitled *The Bi-Polar Express* as a tongue-in-cheek tribute to her father, who is well known in the sport for his fluctuating moods.

By the end of the 2007 season, many fans and racing insiders expect to see Ashley Force's name high up in the NHRA's final points standings and are prepared to see it stay there for many years to come.

Chapter Twenty

Deborah Renshaw

Bowling Green, Kentucky, United States

(1975–)

Not all racers' dreams have happy endings, but while NASCAR Craftsman Truck driver Deborah Renshaw's nightmare of losing her ride came true in 2006, she is still thinking positively about her future behind the wheel.

The 32-year-old native of Bowling Green, Kentucky, began dreaming about racing as a youngster while attending local dirt track races around Kentucky and Tennessee, where her father, Dan, was a race team owner. Deborah, always an eager student of the sport, went to races with her father and helped him record lap times, measure tire pressures and pretty much anything else her little 10-year-old hands could handle.

With her family so heavily invested in the sport, a career in the auto racing industry was somewhat inevitable, so when Deborah attended Northwood University in Michigan, she took automotive marketing and earned an associates degree as well as a bachelors degree in Business, graduating in 1997. Armed with a pocket full of credentials, Deborah started her chase of the checkered flag with the support of her family as she competed at local tracks around Nashville, Tennessee.

Between 1999 and 2000, Deborah competed in the Late Model stock car division at Highland Rim Speedway in Tennessee, where she finished a respectable fifth in the points standing and was runner-up for the Rookie of the Year award. The next season, she participated in NASCAR's Weekly Racing Series at the famed Nashville Speedway USA and the Riverview Speedway, Tennessee. Deborah had 27 starts throughout the season, scoring three top-10 finishes, six top-15 finishes and even one pole at Riverview. At Nashville Superspeedway, Deborah finally found herself at the top of the championship point standings, making history in the process by becoming the first female to lead the points race in a NASCAR-sanctioned series.

In 2002, Renshaw had moved up to the Automobile Racing Club of America (ARCA), but a terrible crash at Loews Motor Speedway, North Carolina, in October ended with the death of fellow racer Eric Martin and nearly finished Renshaw's career. During the practice session for the EasyCare 150, Martin's No.2 Chevrolet spun out as he came off the fourth turn; several other drivers managed to steer past Martin as he came to a full stop perpendicular to the outside wall, facing down the banking. At the time, it wasn't mandatory for spotters to be working during practice sessions, so Renshaw was blithely unaware of Martin's car as she tore around the corner.

She came out of the turn and ploughed her No.75 Ford straight into Martin's Chevy, t-boning his car right on the driver's side as he sat talking to his pit crew, letting them know he was okay; he was dead before he reached the hospital. Although her own injuries were not life-threatening, Deborah was treated at the infield hospital for multiple breaks in her leg as well as severe shock, and as a direct result of the crash NASCAR immediately mandated that spotters be present during all future practice sessions.

After recovering, which took several months of convalescence, Renshaw returned to the 2003 ARCA RE/MAX Series and impressed many onlookers with a flurry of top-10 starts, completing the season with three top-10 finishes.

She moved up the ladder in 2004 to the Craftsman Truck Series, one of the prestigious NASCAR series that is also a major steppingstone to the Nextel Cup. She started 14 out of the 15 races she entered, driving the No.29 Ford F-150 for K Automotive

Racing. She earned two top-20 finishes with a career-best finish of 15th at Martinsville Speedway late in the season, but the big payoff came at Darlington Raceway when Deborah Renshaw became the first female to lead a lap in a NASCAR Craftsman Truck Series race.

In December 2004, she joined the driver development program at Bobby Hamilton Racing (BHR). When she replaced Chase Montgomery in the No.8 truck, Deborah became the first woman to ever run a complete schedule in one of NASCAR's three premier series. The following year, she missed just one race in the season, but delivered two top-10 starts; and under Nextel Cup star Kevin Harvick's mentoring, she finished 12th at Dover and qualified eighth at Nashville. Unfortunately, she failed to score any top-10 finishes and came in a disappointing 24th in the final points standing.

When BHR's primary sponsor, EasyCare, dropped out of the truck series, the team went in search of a replacement. They also replaced their No.8 driver when it was announced that Bobby Hamilton Jr. would run a limited schedule in the truck for the 2006 season and Chase Montgomery would be back behind the wheel for the first race at Daytona. Deborah Renshaw was left high and dry without a ride and without a team, effectively ending her career.

Deborah recently graduated from the National Automobile Dealers Association (NADA) Dealer Candidate Academy, which suggests that she may pursue sales and marketing opportunities in the future if she isn't successful in re-securing a ride. She also made a guest appearance in a country music video "Dare to Dream" by recording star Jo Dee Messina. It seems like Deborah Renshaw is a busy lady, with or without wheels.

In December 2006, Deborah married Shawn Parker, her former pit crew chief, so although Deborah's racing dream may currently be on hold, she still managed to find a happy ending to this chapter of her life.

Chapter Twenty-One

Jutta Kleinschmidt

Cologne, Germany

(1962–)

Legendary Dakar Rally Driver

On January 21, 2001, history was made at the Paris-Dakar rally. For the first time in its 23-year history, a woman had won the toughest rally in the world. German-born Jutta Kleinschmidt took first place in the rally, the crowning jewel in an extraordinary career that saw her drive across some of the toughest terrain on the planet, battling geographical barriers as well as the gender barriers inherent in the male-dominated sport of rally driving.

Later that same year, Kleinschmidt also went on to win the Italian Baja rally and was quickly snapped up by Volkswagen to anchor its cross-country rallying division while also working between races on Volkswagen vehicle development projects. Kleinschmidt eventually drove

VW's exciting new vehicle, the Race-Touareg, to a third-place finish at the 2005 Dakar, capturing the first-ever podium at the famous event in a diesel-powered car. Kleinschmidt's composure out of the car as well as her skill behind the wheel has made her a formidable contender and a proven winner.

Born in 1962 in Cologne, Germany, Jutta was originally interested in motorbikes, and in 1987, she found herself avidly following the exciting Dakar rally while on holiday. It was that close-up experience that ignited her passion for rally racing. That same year, she rode in her first desert rally, the Pharaohs Rally in Egypt, and in 1988, she started her first Dakar Rally on a motorbike.

Kleinschmidt studied general physics in university, but after graduating she decided to pursue a dual career. She secured a position in BMW's development department while also competing in marathon races, first in motorbike races. After six years, she left BMW altogether to focus her attention on motor racing.

The winning began in 1992 with a first-place Ladies Cup in Paris–Cape Town Rally and the Pharaohs Rally, as well as the 24-Hour race at Clermont-Ferrand, all on motorbike. She also participated in car rallying that same year at the Nürburgring and Spa 24-Hour races.

Between 1993 and 1996, the German slowly shifted from two to four wheels before finally making a car her full-time race vehicle, but not before she tasted victory with several podium finishes in consecutive Pharaohs Rallies and a first-place finish in the 1994 Ladies Cup at the Paris–Dakar Rally. Her experiences during those early Enduro motorbike races gave her the opportunity to get to know the landscape of each of the big rally tracks, especially the Dakar course.

Racing on a motorbike requires frequent spells of riding standing up, which offers a clearer view of the track in every direction. Motorbike racers must learn to ride a clean line in order to avoid hazards that usually go unseen from inside the cockpit of a car or truck. This intimate course knowledge paid off big time for Jutta when she switched rides to a car: having navigated the courses from the seat of a motorbike, Jutta knew every dip and groove of the road. The Dakar Rally, for example, is especially notorious for its treacherous terrain in the North African portion of the rally, and even innocent-looking clumps of grass or sand dunes have caused deadly crashes.

What also contributed to Kleinschmidt's strength at driving in the desert was her tireless work ethic, her meticulousness and her extensive technical knowledge. She understood the workings of her car, and during all pre-race testing, she noted every detail, constantly asking questions of her mechanics and then analyzing the data as an engineer would.

Her diligence and knowledge has resulted in many records and groundbreaking drives for Kleinschmidt. In 1997, she was the first woman to win a Dakar rally stage, and in 1999, she was the first woman to lead. That same year, Jutta took the podium in numerous events, including a fourth place in the Italian Baja, a fourth place in the Tunisia Rally, a third place in the United Arab Emirates (UAE) Desert Challenge and a fourth place in the World Cup for Cross Country Rallies. She also captured third place overall in the Granada–Dakar Rally and notched two stage wins; in addition, she was the first-ever woman to lead in this event (from third to fifth stage) and the first-ever woman to score a podium finish in this rally. Add to that a respectable seventh-place finish in the Nürburgring 24-Hour race with teammates Ellen Lohr and Claudia Hürtgen (Carlsson Mercedes-Benz SLK), as well as a class win in the Veedol Endurance Cup (Mitsubishi GDI Carisma).

Between 2000 and 2005, Jutta was almost unstoppable. As works driver for Mitsubishi Germany (Mitsubishi Pajero T2), Jutta scored a fifth place in the Paris–Dakar–Cairo Rally, a second in the Tunisia Rally, a fourth in the Morocco Rally, and second-place finishes in the Baja Espana Master Rally and the Por Las Pampas Rally. She also logged a sixth place in the UAE Desert Challenge and ended the season in second place overall in the final standings of the 2000 World Cup for Cross Country Rallies. As of March 2001, Jutta also competed as the works driver for Mitsubishi Motors Japan, and yet another year of outstanding performances secured Jutta a second-place finish in the final standings of the 2001 World Cup for Cross Country Rallies.

The accolades kept rolling in throughout 2001: Kleinschmidt was awarded the Engineers in Motion title by the Association of German Engineers (VDI) and was voted Allgemeiner Deutscher Automobil-Club (ADAC) Motor Sports Personality of the Year, as well as the ARD Sports Personality of the Year by TV viewers. She was also voted Rally Driver of the Year by *Motorsport Aktuell* magazine's readership and received the Lord Wakefield Trophy from the British Women Racing Driver's Club as Outstanding Lady Competitor.

In May 2002, she signed a new three-year contract with Volkswagen that would not only see her behind the wheel, but also heavily involved with the development process of a new diesel-powered rally vehicle.

In 2003, Jutta was paired with co-driver Fabrizia Pons in the Volkswagen Tarek, and they took eighth overall in the Telefónica–Dakar Rally, placing second in their class (two-wheel drive vehicles). She closed out the season with a seventh overall in the Italian Baja and a third overall Baja Deutschland, placing first in her class (two-wheel drive vehicles).

With the introduction of the new VW Touareg in 2004, Jutta and Fabrizia guided the vehicle to a 21st overall in the Telefónica–Dakar Rally, and with co-driver Bobby Willis, she finished fourth in the Morocco Rally. Jutta then placed third overall in the Rallye d'Orient and 13th in the UAE Desert Challenge.

With Fabrizia co-driving again in 2005, Jutta placed third overall in the Telefónica–Dakar and Por Las Pampas rallies, fourth overall in the Tunisian Rally, then third overall in the Moroccan Rally and second overall at Baja Portalegre.

With Lisbon as the new starting point for the 2006 Dakar, Jutta was keen to get her 15th rally start under way. Unfortunately, she did not visit the podium, having to pull out during the 11th stage after hitting a series of potholes and damaging her car's steering, frame and suspension. Not only did this mark the end of the rally for Jutta, it also marked the end of her relationship with Volkswagen.

In early February 2006, Kleinschmidt left Volkswagen after failing to come to terms with the VW team to extend her contract, which had expired January 31. The 43-year-old had been pivotal in accelerating Volkswagen's technical and mechanical developments and was personally responsible their recent Rally Raid success. However, just days after those contract talks between Kleinschmidt and Volkswagen fell through, Kleinschmidt confirmed she was set to join the X-Raid BMW team. Jutta was joined by new teammates Nasser Al-Attiyah of Qatar and Guerlain Chicherit of France for the 2007 Dakar. Just prior to that race Jutta will compete the UAE Desert Challenge (held November 5–11), which will give her a great opportunity to get up to speed with her new ride, the BMW X3. Partnered with new co-driver Tina Thörner, the dunes of the United Arab Emirates gives them the chance to work out vital cockpit communications, the drivers' "shorthand," before the more exacting Dakar course several weeks later.

Jutta has more than proven her ability to succeed in the traditionally male-dominated domains of rally racing, engineering and auto design and development; she even completed her exams at a boys' secondary school in Freilassing in 1980. Jutta recently joined the lucrative motivational speaking circuit in Europe and speaks about subjects such as teamwork, crisis management, working under pressure and goal achievement.

Ever the consummate athlete, Jutta once rode across the continental United States on a bicycle in the "Race Across America" event, a feat suitable for only the most well-trained and mentally-strong among us. She regularly enjoys long cycle tours, such as the 1500 kilometer Alp crossing, and also participates in other, less strenuous off-season sporting activities while she relaxes at her home in Monaco. She has even decided to try to conquer the air and has acquired her helicopter license. But there is little time for these hobbies during her Dakar preparations as Jutta intensifies her training program by cycling to increase stamina, regularly doing weight training and go-karting, which apparently is good for back muscles and concentration. With her personal trainer, Jean-Jacques Rivet, she tests her coordination and balance on specially designed machines.

Jutta's enthusiasm and attitude remains buoyant. She has been quoted as saying, "Cross-country rallying is a fantastic cocktail of adventure, technology and racing, and the Dakar is the challenge of the year for me, for which I have worked 11 long months." The Dakar is not just another race and Jutta Kleinschmidt is not just another race driver—she is one of the sport's greatest endurance rally racers.

Chapter Twenty-Two

Melanie Troxel

Littleton, Colorado, United States

(1972–)

M elanie Troxel is one fast lady. By clocking a 4.458 second pass and a top speed of 330.31 miles per hour, she became the quickest female driver in NHRA history on the Dallas drag strip in 2005. Since then, she has increased her record speed to a staggering 331.04 miles per hour.

The daughter of veteran drag racer and 1988 NHRA Alcohol Dragster champion Mike Troxel, Melanie grew up in Colorado working on airplanes with her father. Those early days instilled a strict work ethic in the youngster, who inherited her father's passion for fast cars and for the sport of drag racing. With such a great teacher, it was no surprise that at age 16, when she was just old enough to get her racing license, Melanie ran her first drag race in a car powered by an engine she rebuilt herself.

Encouraged by both her father and mother Barbara, Melanie completed her education and immediately began her professional career in 1997, racing a Top Alcohol dragster. Within two years, she had captured two NHRA national event victories at Seattle and Topeka and was ready to step up to the Top Fuel dragster class, signing with Don Schumacher Racing in 2000.

That year, she scored one runner-up finish at Dallas before deciding to take a short break, running a limited Top Fuel schedule in 2002 and 2003. Don Schumacher Racing gave her the ride she was looking for to re-launch her career in 2005, and Melanie did not disappoint. After 11 races in the 2005 season, Melanie had already scored eight round wins and finished out the season with a runner-up finish at Pomona.

When the 2006 season started, Melanie was in great form, opening with her first career Top Fuel victory, followed a few weeks later by a second in Las Vegas. She subsequently became the first NHRA Top Fuel driver to reach the final round in the first five events of a season. Melanie continued to impress by leading the point standings through the first 12 events. She charmed the sports media too, especially *Speed Magazine* who named her 2006 First Quarter Driver of the Year, beating out the big boys of NASCAR including future 2006 Nextel Cup champion, Jimmie Johnson, and IRL's fan favorite, Helio Castroneves.

By October 2006, the NHRA POWERade Series driver had advanced to a Top Fuel best eight final rounds, and she was honored with the Sportswoman of the Year award by the Billie Jean King Women's Sports Foundation. Previous award winners included female athletes from around the world in tennis, skating and golf, but Troxel was the first auto racer to ever win the award. Melanie was also awarded the USAC's Kara Hendrick Spirit Award, which honors female drivers for their spirit, determination and driving ability.

By the end of the season, ESPN honored Melanie with two ESPY awards nominations—one for Female Athlete of the Year and a second for Driver of the Year, the first time in NHRA history that a driver has been given a double nomination in two separate categories. She closed out her first full Top Fuel season with a respectable fourth-place finish, 210 points behind teammate Tony Schumacher but with the distinction of two event wins (Pomona and Las Vegas) under her belt.

As the 2007 season dawned, Melanie had a brand new sponsor and began racing in the Vietnam Veterans Memorial/POW-MIA dragster, with her first victory of the year coming in St. Louis where she scored her third Top Fuel career win in the 330 miles per hour competitive NHRA world. Her confidence on the track certainly proves that she's ready to compete for the 2007 Top Fuel Championship.

Not content with merely developing her on-track profile, in June 2007 Melanie and her husband, Funny Car driver Tommy Johnson Jr., signed a deal with ESPN to create and to host a new reality-based half-hour ESPN drag racing program entitled *King of the Strip*. Melanie also continues to operate her specialty automotive tool shop, supplying tools to race teams and machine shops.

Melanie and Tommy currently live in Avon, Indiana, where they both enjoy playing golf and snowboarding when they're not hurtling down the drag strips.

Chapter Twenty-Three

Hillary Will

Fortuna, California, United States
(1980–)

Hillary Will has the perfect drag racing pedigree. The oldest of five children, she has been influenced by both her father, Steve, and her grandfather, Connie, who regularly took the family out to watch drag racers compete against the clock.

In 1996, Hillary's father gave her a '73 Dodge Challenger for her 16th birthday to get her to and from high school. One day, her father suggested they take the Challenger down to the local quarter-mile track, just to see how fast she could go; and so was born a speed queen.

Until that point, Hillary had only ever watched her dad from the sidelines. Steve raced extensively throughout the '70s and early '80s, but when Hillary and the rest of the brood started arriving, he gave it up in order to work a safer job that could better support his family.

With Steve's help, Hillary began bracket racing, which is a form of drag racing that allows for a handicap, or dial-in time, between the predicted speeds of each of the two cars. As her experience grew, her dad put her in a faster car and she started racing the Super Street series. After spending her first post-secondary year at Wheaton College in Massachusetts, Hillary came home to California for a summer of racing and began winning race after race.

She continued to spend her summers drag racing, but upon graduating magna cum laude with a degree in economics and winning the prestigious Wall Street Journal Student Achievement Award, she decided to pursue a more traditional career as a financial analyst. Nevertheless she still spent every last cent of her savings on racing, taking lessons at the Frank Hawley NHRA Drag Racing School in Florida. In 1999, however, when Hillary went to the finals at Sonoma and had a taste of the excitement, she knew that she was never going to be able to stop racing.

She quickly moved up the ladder into faster categories, then jumped to Super Gas and Super Comp before moving to Top Alcohol Dragster (TAD) in 2004 after receiving her TAD license from Frank Hawley's Florida school.

In April 2005, she made the decision to go for broke and make racing her full-time career. She quit her financial analyst job and focused 100 percent of her time on securing corporate sponsorship for her Top Alcohol team, hoping to bring in enough money to eventually compete at the pro racing level.

Running a supercharged engine in the TAD circuit, Hillary won one divisional race and finished the 2005 race season in second place competing in Division 6. She was also one of only four drivers of supercharged alcohol dragsters to exceed 270 miles per hour that year. Hillary finished sixth in the national points standing, winning the spring SummitRacing.com Nationals in Las Vegas where she was the number one qualifier, setting the lowest-elapsed time record and registering the top speed of the race. She also finished runner-up in two other events, the Winternationals in Pomona and the Mac Tools U.S. Nationals in Indianapolis.

Throughout 2004 and 2005, Hillary's TAD records included two first-place qualifying spots, two lowest-elapsed times and four top speeds. To date, her career best stats in TAD are a lowest-elapsed time of 4.58 seconds and a top speed of 326 miles per hour, driving Doug Kalitta's Top Fueler.

In recent years, Hillary has worked with some of the greats in drag racing, improving her game to the point that she is now well on the path to becoming a racing great. As part of the prestigious Kalitta Motorsports team, she learned how to win in the Top Alcohol division from Bucky Austin, a 17-time national event champion and well-respected personality in the racing world. Most recently, Hillary has benefited from the knowledge and experience imparted to her by the legendary Shirley Muldowney, who is the wife of Kalitta crew chief Rahn Tobler. She also has the unswerving support of her father and grandfather.

Chapter Twenty-Four

Laleh Seddigh

Tehran, Iran

(1977–)

When you think of countries that support and nurture female auto racers, Iran would probably be somewhere near the bottom of the list. But Iran's talented and glamorous Laleh Seddigh loves speed as much as she loves a challenge and spends as much time breaking cultural stereotypes as she does racing records.

In the fall of 2004, Ms. Seddigh petitioned the national auto racing federation in the male-dominated society of Iran for permission to compete against men, and much to everyone's surprise, permission was granted. She not only became the first woman in Iran to race cars against the opposite sex, but also the first woman since the Islamic Revolution to compete against men in any sport. And what's more, she beat 'em!

A PhD student from Tehran, Seddigh is considered one of the most promising woman drivers ever from Iran, and her driving skills have earned her the nickname "Little Schumacher" after the recently retired German Formula One champion. While she agrees that competing with men is not easy, especially in Iran, she is often quoted as saying that she hopes her example will encourage other women to follow suit.

She has inspired some 30 other women drivers to compete; however, these ladies are still not allowed to compete in the same category as men like Seddigh is, and women's awards are still given separately. It hasn't been an easy ride for Seddigh, though; when she recently won the national championship and the whole nation seemed ready to cheer, the Islamic Republic of Iran Broadcasting (IRIB) refused to show her on the victory podium elevated above the men. Thankfully, there was a plethora of newsprint photographers there to capture the historic moment as the new champ stood quietly to receive her medal, and as she had promised the race organizers, Seddigh wore a scarf over her long dark hair as well as a long coat to hide her racing uniform.

It has only been in the past few years that women have even been allowed to watch men's sports, and even then they are kept segregated, relegated to distant viewing stands. During Seddigh's first race, the women screamed and climbed up the fences to show their joy, and this worried the race organizers. After completing the race, Seddigh had to promise not to wave or even acknowledge the crowd, a third of whom were women.

The oldest of four children, her open-minded father taught her to drive on weekends in a park on the outskirts of Tehran when she was 13 years old. Ten years later, she started racing miniature race cars that resembled go-karts. She also entered numerous three-day cross-country rallies, changing her own tires and doing all her own repair work; but don't think all this racing bravado was without danger. Laleh broke her neck in one accident and her left leg in another wreck. That leg is now held together by metal screws.

She has even wrecked a couple of family cars on the city streets. The chaotic traffic of Tehran makes competitive drivers of even the humblest of commuters. The traffic lights count down the seconds before turning green, creating a palpable racetrack feel, and Seddigh is not immune to the occasional drag race during shopping expeditions.

When Iran's racing federation appointed a new president, Mohammad Khatami, who was more inclined to allow women to enter the men's races, Laleh finally got her opportunity to compete against the boys. Although there was considerable jealousy and animosity from many of the male drivers, others like Saeed Arabian, the previous

Iranian national racing champion who is now Seddigh's coach, are proud of what she has achieved and they celebrate her bravery.

For most of her life, Laleh has been pushing against the barriers of those traditionally male pursuits. Laleh was fortunate to have an enlightened and encouraging father, and she has spent her academic career in preparation to succeed him in the family business, receiving a bachelor's degree in industrial management and a master's in production engineering. Apart from her busy racing schedule, she works a day job as the managing director of a company that produces spare car parts.

Ms. Seddigh is a shining symbol for a whole generation of young Iranians who are constantly testing their social, political and religious boundaries. Seventy percent of Iranians are under 35, and they have, with some gentle persuasion, quietly succeeded in securing freedoms unimaginable even a few years ago. For the women of Tehran, at least, head scarves are now often brightly colored and worn loosely over the hair, and the obligatory overcoats can now have a more tailored and flattering appearance.

Until 2005, Ms. Seddigh was sponsored by Proton, an Iranian-assembled Malaysian car company, but lately more prestigious international sponsors are taking notice and could inject much-needed funding into the sport. She has been offered a Subaru sponsorship and has fielded offers from Mazda and Hyundai, but accepting any of these would necessitate her moving away from Iran, a move which she is not yet ready to make. She will have to make that decision one day, however, because auto racing in Iran can offer her only modest rewards: all her victories to date have resulted in a few medals, a cup and some certificates of achievement—hardly enough to base a racing career on.

In March 2006, Ms. Seddigh was finally awarded her International Racing Driving License during the BMW School Series at the Bahrain International Circuit in Manama, opening up more options for her. She now teaches a training class for women race-car drivers, the first in the country, but every time Laleh needs to practice or conduct testing, the track staff demand she secure a letter of permission. The male drivers are never required to comply and aren't usually even asked for such validation.

Even with the numerous restrictions imposed by racing authorities and her constant omission from Iran's highly conservative sports newscasts, Laleh Seddigh's name is becoming well known to western journalists and race fans. Hopefully she'll soon be seen racing on international circuits proudly representing Iran.

Chapter Twenty-Five

Leilani Münter

Rochester, Minnesota, United States

(1976–)

Five-foot four-inch Minnesota-born Leilani Münter is not only at home behind the wheel of a race car, but she's also adept at handling a microphone as a trackside reporter for NASCAR.com. And if anyone wants to learn how to drive like Earnhardt or Gordon, Leilani's your girl; she's also an instructor at the Fast Track High Performance Racing School in Harrisburg, North Carolina, not far from the city of Cornelius where she currently resides.

But four-wheeled mechanical beasts aren't the only interests in her life. Münter has also received her bachelor's degree in biology from the University of California San Diego and became a teacher's assistant in Cellular and Developmental Biology, earning the Presidential Academic Fitness Award. And if that isn't enough, this academic young woman has photo- and stunt-doubled for Hollywood superstar Catherine Zeta-Jones, whom she resembles so closely that they could be twins. She has also done stand-in work for Salma Hayek, performed stunts for the film *The Scorpion King*, as well as worked on camera in George Clooney's *Ocean's Eleven* and in the Kate Hudson movie *Almost Famous*.

Thirty-year-old Leilani is half German and half Japanese/Hawaiian, which accounts for both her exotic looks and her name. Her parents both worked in the medical profession and she has three older sisters, one of whom, Natascha, is married to Bob Weir, founding guitarist for the Grateful Dead.

But even with such a high-powered family, Leilani was able to stake her own claim to fame by setting a lot of records in the racing world; and that all began just as the world moved into the new millennium.

Münter began racing stock cars seriously in 2000, and in 2001 she competed in the Allison Legacy Series. She then moved to North Carolina in 2002 to get closer to the action and maybe fulfill her dreams of becoming a professional racer. Not wanting to be thought of as just another pretty girl hanging out with the boys, she picked up a set of tools and got to work in body shops and as a crewmember in race shops, doing the menial jobs such as bathroom duty as well as helping to build racing shocks. This hands-on experience taught her a different side of the sport, and she soon realized that it wasn't just about the driver turning left and driving as fast as they could: winning was the result of a real team effort.

During her workshop days, Leilani tested late models and studied race-car setup, geometry and aerodynamics under the tutelage of Larry McReynolds, the former Winston Cup crew chief for the late Dale Earnhardt Sr.. Her beauty and charm also won her lots of off-track attention, such as when *Esquire* named her one of their "Women We Love" in the April 2002 issue. In the October 2003 edition of *Men's Journal*, Leilani was given the title of "America's Sexiest Race Car Driver." *FHM* magazine ran a five-page spread of photos along with an interview in the September 2003 issue, and she was subsequently dubbed "The Hottest Woman in NASCAR."

But Leilani Münter just wanted to race. From the first time she got behind the wheel of a race car, Leilani knew her life would be focused on racing. She has been quoted as saying that her first ride in a stock car "was a very defining moment for me, because my entire life changed that day. There were no questions, no doubts…it was all I wanted to do, all I could think about."

As she pursued her dream, she spent countless hours searching for sponsors while also driving every second she could. Fortunately for her, she entered the sport as it was transitioning from the traditional old boys club to a more inclusive environment where women were now being sponsored by more teams and larger corporations. In the scant handful of years that she's been racing, Leilani has already successfully secured the backing of two major sponsors: Hostess Twinkies, on whose box her face appears as one of three "Hostess Race Divas" (Danica Patrick and Melanie Troxel being the other "divas"), and Konica Minolta Printing Solutions, for whom Leilani acts as driver and spokesperson.

In 2003, Münter signed on as a developmental driver in a multi-year deal with Team Bristol Motorsports and worked on their No.54 Busch series team from January through April until the late model racing season started. However, after her successful top-10 debut in the NASCAR Weekly Racing Series Late Model division, the team went bankrupt. The disappointment was palpable, but being the trooper she is Leilani just looked at it as just another bump in the road to her inevitable success and started all over again.

Moving forward the next year, Leilani debuted in the ROMCO Super Late Model Series with an impressive performance, coming in sixth fastest out of 26 race cars during the practice session and then went on to set the record for highest-ever qualifying position by a female driver at the Texas Motor Speedway. Her sponsorship, now including *FHM* magazine, grew when Trimspa came onboard and sponsored her for a NASCAR Elite division race at Kentucky Speedway, after which NASCAR.com came knocking and offered her the position of special correspondent. High-profile media attention followed, along with a cover shoot for *Corvette Quarterly* magazine and a hosting stint on Spike TV.

As the 2005 season began, Leilani started working as an instructor for the Fast Track High Performance Driving School, giving ride-alongs and lessons at Lowe's Motor Speedway, the Nashville SuperSpeedway, the Kentucky Speedway and the Atlanta Motor Speedway. She also scored even more media attention on television with a feature on *NASCAR Nation* and in print with a cover shot in *Rochester* Magazine, as well as being profiled in the photography book *A Day in the Life of the American Woman*.

She marked her first full-time season of racing in 2006 with a combination of rides in the ASA, USRA and NASCAR Elite Division for the SS Racing team in Indianapolis. Then in June 2006, she returned to the Texas track, this time setting the record for the highest finishing position for a female driver when she claimed fourth place in the Konica Minolta 100. She added yet another entry to the record books three months later when she became the first woman to qualify in the 45-year history of the Bettenhausen Classic at Illiana Speedway, Indiana. She also competed in a late model race in Wisconsin that year, racing against established short track racers including NASCAR Champions Tony Stewart and Matt Kenseth and posting a time that was 0.3 seconds off of Stewart's quickest time. ESPN took notice and started filming Leilani's progress; the documentary, entitled *ESPN Ultimate NASCAR: The Explosion* aired on the network in July 2007. She gained even more front-page recognition when her photo appeared on the home page of FOXSports.com and the cover of *Speedworld* magazine.

Leilani moved into a national series in 2007 and competed in the ARCA RE/MAX Series, which was her first time competing with live national television exposure. At the start of the season, she completed her rookie test at Daytona International Speedway in an ARCA car, and after just two practice runs, she proved her worth by logging a lap at 177.644 miles per hour, the 24th quickest of a field of 59 cars testing. She also renewed her sponsorship deal with Hostess for a second year, appearing on boxes of Hostess Twinkies, Cupcakes and Donettes.

But do not think of Leilani Münter as any kind of "twinkie." She understands the obstacles faced by women entering the racing arena and is determined to become a role model for other young women coming into the sport. Apart from the usual quests for respect on the track, for sponsorships and for the best equipment available, she knows that women face the bigger barrier of being stereotyped as weaker and less competitive than their male opponents. Leilani understands that there will always be a few people who will never change their minds about women in racing and that you can't win them all over.

Her fans remain supportive, and sponsors are starting to notice the increased marketing value of having a woman in the driver's seat. Leilani, for her part, makes sure that rigorous workouts and training sessions keep her in that position; also, in order to condition herself for the physical demands of driving a race car, she does bikram "hot" yoga several times a week. Working out for over an hour in a humid room heated to 100 degrees Fahrenheit helps build up her body's heat tolerance and strength, a much needed asset when sitting in a hot car for periods of up to four hours on sun-baked tracks. She spends a lot of time in the swimming pool too, and whenever she gets the chance, she loves to scuba dive and go snowboarding. Her diet consists of mostly vegetarian foods containing lots of protein and meat substitutes.

She also has a good handle on her personal life and has been dating her current boyfriend for nearly three years. Her beau has nothing to do with racing, however, as she tries to keep her off-track activities out of the public eye. But Leilani is public about her passion for charities and other worthy causes, and she has lent her name to or volunteered for the World Wildlife Federation, the Elephant Sanctuary and the Black Beauty Ranch. A staunch animal lover, she also volunteered for at a wildlife rehabilitation center while attending college.

She has said on many occasions that she tries to race clean, always giving the other drivers space on the track. She wants to beat them fair and square through speed and skill, not by putting them into the wall, a relatively professional and mature attitude for a rookie driver to have. As her racing career evolves, Leilani is sure to continue to impress both on and off the track.

Chapter Twenty-Six

FAST LADIES OF THE FUTURE

A number of women racers have emerged in recent years whose names will most likely appear in future auto racing record books. Keep your eye on these ladies and remember, you heard about them here first!

I. Mishael Abbott (1981–)

Born in Jefferson City, Missouri, Mishael currently drives in the Indy Pro series and the Sports Car Club of America road series. She drove her first race in 1995, participating in the Yamaha Junior Restricted series (World Karting Association), and her first victory came in 1996 in that same WKA series.

Mishael also won her first WKA Championship in 1996 and set a record as the first female to win an SKUSA feature event. Her racing heroes include Al Unser Jr. and Greg Moore, as well as early women's racing legend Janet Guthrie, whose record-shattering career helped women break into the male-dominated sport back in the early '70s. Mishael's ultimate goal is to be the first female driver to win the Indy 500.

She is currently pursuing dual degrees from the Florida Atlantic University in elementary education and the University of Indianapolis in sports marketing.

II. Mary Katherine (1966–)

Born in Milwaukee, Wisconsin, this petite 5'4" mother of five currently resides in South Florida. Ever since she was a little girl, Mary had dreamed of being a race-car driver; instead of dolls and teddy bears, she played with Matchbox cars, pretending that she was racing in them at over 100 miles per hour. As one of 10 children, she spent most of her play time with her brothers watching cars speed around the tracks on television.

As a teen, she attended two Indianapolis 500s, but her dream of becoming a race-car driver was put on hold when, at 19, she married her high school sweetheart, and the young couple moved to Arkansas to become cotton farmers. There, Mary learned to drive a tractor, hardly an Indy qualifier, but after eight years of farming, she and her husband moved to South Florida with their newborn daughter, Nancy. While training and working as a pastry chef, Mary gave birth to four more daughters, but shortly after her youngest was born, her husband of 17 years left the marriage. Suddenly, at 36, she was a single mother raising five young daughters, so Mary decided to gamble everything she had on her old dream. She found a racing school near her home and started taking lessons to become a pro racer.

After three seasons in the ultra-competitive Spec Miata class and several top-five finishes, Mary was ready for the big show. In February 2006, she officially became a professional race-car driver, signing on with the Tindol Motorsports team to drive in the World Challenge touring car series. Her Mazda Protégé carries a few modifications, but is basically the same vehicle you would find in your local dealer's showroom.

Mary is keen to represent both the team and women drivers in general in a pro series, and her daughters—Nancy, 13, Maggie, 11, Lane, 10, Mia, 6, and Helen, 4—are her biggest and most vocal fans at the track. During her off-track downtime, Mary also enjoys speaking to school children about safety issues and addresses numerous women's groups on various subjects, including marital abandonment and how to get on with your life. Mary Katharine is the perfect role model for any woman wanting to create a life for herself on her own terms, and she brings a sense of honesty as well as her great sense of humor to her various speaking engagements.

III. Michelle Theriault (1986–)

Currently the driver of the Team Glock Racing No.37 Chevrolet Monte Carlo SS, this Connecticut native started racing in 1992 at the age of six, competing in Quarter Midgets. As a toddler, her father, Dave, used to take her with him to watch family friends race miniature speedsters at local racetracks. When she was five, Michelle saw a race car with a "for sale" sign stuck on it and begged to sit in it. No sooner had she plopped down into the seat than she turned to her daddy and said, "I want this"; and so her future was sealed.

Over the next seven years, she proved to be a natural at the sport, scoring more than 200 wins across 13 states and finishing runner-up in the Quarter Midgets of America National Championship five times.

In 1999, the entire Theriault family relocated to Georgia in order for Michelle to learn and race alongside the pros. She soon moved up from

Quarter Midgets to Legends Cars where she again excelled, winning the Atlanta Motor Speedway's Thunder Racing Legends Championship, becoming the first woman Legends Car Champion.

Two more championships followed, along with more than 20 race wins, and after three years running in Legends Car, Theriault graduated to Late Models in 2003 and finished well in all 20 of her events. She placed sixth in the series championship and was also named runner-up to the Rookie of the Year. That same season, she competed in two NASCAR Dodge Weekly Series Super Late Model Division races (Lanier National Speedway and Music City Motorplex).

In 2004, Theriault entered the United Speed Alliance Racing (USAR) Hooters ProCup Series, and not only was she the only woman competing in the series, Michelle also became the first woman to qualify for the National Championship.

During that period, she was invited to participate in Ford Racing's Driver Development program, which evaluated and mentored young up-and-coming drivers both on and off the track.

In May 2004, Michelle graduated from high school with an impressive 4.0 GPA, but while her classmates were busy celebrating their scholastic freedom and entry into adulthood, Michelle was busy filming a reality-based TV series *The Drive* for Country Music Television (CMT). The series featured seven race-car drivers as they went about their daily lives and dealt with the stress and excitement of stock car racing.

Theriault debuted in the NASCAR Grand National Division West Series in 2005 and again qualified for the USAR Hooters ProCup Series National Championship for the second year in a row. She impressed sports industry insiders over the following season with her enthusiasm, track skills and commitment to push through all obstacles that got in the way of her reaching the checkered flag ahead of the pack. The 2007 season marked her rookie year in the Busch East Series, although her previous success behind the wheel eluded her, with no wins or top-five finishes to date. Michelle is also racing in the ARCA RE/MAX series and is hopeful her luck will return by the end of the season.

With Dale Earnhardt as her racing hero, Michelle Theriault is focused on a long and exciting career in NASCAR, and with the help of her well-seasoned race team and the support of her family, she may just get the opportunity to become the first woman to win the Nextel Cup. Michelle is certainly keeping her eyes on the prize.

IV. Simona De Silvestro (1988–)

Driving the Walker Racing Team's No.5 Miauton in the Champ Car Atlantic Series, this brilliant young racer currently resides in Mont sur Rolle, Switzerland, and has proven herself a real contender, adding off-track style to her on-track competitive attitude.

In 2006, she completed her first season in the Formula BMW USA championship, claiming one win, six podium finishes and 11 top-10s out of 14 races. This gave Simona a fourth-place finish in the overall point standings—not bad for the young rookie. When she claimed a podium finish in Indianapolis, she became the first-ever woman to get on the podium in Indianapolis Motor Speedway history.

Born in 1988, the teen sensation has been a fan of auto racing all of her life. The only child of a car dealer in Thun, Switzerland, Simona's father, Pierluigi, took his three-year-old daughter to go-kart shows, sitting her on his lap behind the wheel and letting her steer. Simona spent her weekends watching Formula One races with her father, and when she was four years old, Pierluigi took her to her first F1 race at Spa. Even at that young age, Simona knew exactly what she wanted to be when she grew up: a race car driver. The first words she ever said as a baby were "Daddy, Mommy, Ferrari and Prost."

With the reluctant support of her mother, Emanuela, and the inspiration to race from her father, who was a director of AMAG overseeing the production for Audi and Porsche in Switzerland as well as a Super License driving instructor, De Silvestro got into her first go-kart by the age of six; by age seven, she was already competing in the regional championships. She won her first kart race in 1998, then went on to compete in the Swiss Championship, where she placed seventh in 2002. That same year she placed 13th in the Kart-Cup Monaco and second at the Bridgestone-Cup Switzerland.

The next year De Silvestro saw even more success, starting with a fifth-place finish in the Wintercup Lonato, a second at the Trofeo Industria Parma and a third in the Primavera Lonato. She placed a disappointing 15th in the 2004 French Championship Formula A, followed by a dismal 21st place in the 2005 Formula Renault 2000 Championship in Italy.

The 2006 season was a major turning point for Simona. As she was warming up for the Formula BMW MoSport race in Canada, Walker Racing owner Derrick Walker witnessed her qualifying and race runs. He was impressed with her driving prowess and saw her potential, and shortly thereafter he suggested she test for his Champ Car Atlantic team. After a more than successful test, Simona signed on to campaign the No.5 car throughout the 2007 season with the Indianapolis-based race team.

With all the excitement of her on-track appearances and a full race calendar for 2007, it's surprising to learn that this young lady still finds time to hang out with her friends and continue her education, which includes studying foreign languages—she currently speaks French, German, Italian, Swiss-German and English fluently. In between races during the 2007 season, she spent her downtime playing golf and tennis; she's also currently teaching herself Spanish.

As her lifelong dream is to race in Formula One, perhaps she's one day planning to yell "adios" as she speeds past F1's current Spanish superstar Fernando Alonso?

APPENDIX: IMPORTANT DATES IN WOMEN'S MOTORSPORTS

1899
- Mme. Labrousse becomes the first female racing driver when she enters the Paris–Spa race, finishing fifth in the three-seater class.

1900
- The Ranelagh Club of London, England, organized a Ladies' Race, which is won by a Miss Wemblyn. She competes against only three other women.

1901
- Camille du Gast enters the Paris to Berlin Race and finishes 33rd out of a field of 122 entrants.

1903
- The Ladies Automobile Club of Great Britain and Ireland is formed as an affiliation to, but separate from, the Royal Automobile Club (RAC). The first appointed President of the Ladies Automobile Club is the Duchess of Sutherland.
- Soon-to-be legendary British racer Dorothy Levitt wins her class at the Southport Speed Trials.

1904
- Dorothy Levitt races her De Dion car in the Hereford 1000-mile trial.

1906
- Dorothy Levitt breaks the women's world speed record with an official speed clocked at 96 miles per hour.

1909
- The Women's Motoring Club is formed in the U.S. and their first organized race is an all-female event run from New York to Pennsylvania and back again, with 12 entrants.

1921
- Italian Baroness Maria Antonietta d'Avanso wins the Coppa delle Dame race at the Brescia Speed Week.

1923
- Vincenc "Cenek" Junek gives his wife, Elizabeth Junek, an Italian-made Bugatti Type 30, a car which would soon become her trademark auto.

1924
- The Autodrome de Linas-Montlhéry is built at Montlhéry in France.

1926

- Czech racing pioneer and Bugatti Babe Elizabeth Junek competes in the Targa Florio in Sicily, a race requiring great physical strength. Although her vehicle crashes out of the race, her performance earns her a great deal of respect. She later wins the two-liter sports car class at Nürburgring, Germany, making her the only woman in history to win a Grand Prix race.

1928

- Anne-Cécile Rose-Itier grids for the Grand Prix Féminin at Montlhéry, considered by many to be one of the most prestigious ladies' auto races of the day.

1929

- Hellé Nice, driving an Omega-Six, wins an all-female Grand Prix race at the Montlhéry racetrack, setting a new Women's World Land Speed Record.

1931

- Motorsports fanatic and future romantic novelist Barbara Cartland organizes a women's race at England's famed Brooklands track.
- Gwenda Stewart is renowned as one of the fastest people on three wheels, driving three-wheeled Morgan autos.
- Hellé Nice races a Bugatti T35C in five major Grands Prix in France, as well as in the Italian Grand Prix at Monza.

1933

- Hellé Nice competes in the Italian Grand Prix at the Autodromo Nazionale Monza, a race that would become infamous as one of the most tragic races in GP history and in which three of the world's top racers—Giuseppe Campari, Baconin "Mario Umberto" Borzacchini and the Polish count Stanislas Czaikowski—are all killed in track accidents and crashes.

1935

- Toronto, Canada-born Kay Petre races at the Brooklands course and sets several speed records. On August 6, 1935, Gwenda Stewart takes the ultimate Brooklands Ladies Outer Circuit lap record at 135.95 miles per hour, beating Kay Petre's record set just three days earlier by a mere 0.65 seconds.
- Anne-Cécile and fellow Bugatti driver, Jean Delorme, found the Union Sportive Automobile (USA) for independent drivers who didn't feel that they were being supported and protected by the established French Drivers Association (AGACI).

1936

- Hellé Nice crashes while racing in Brazil and, after a seemingly miraculous recovery, becomes something of a national hero to the Brazilians; many families even name their newborn daughters "Helenice" after her.

1939

- Jean Bugatti is killed while testing one of his company's vehicles, crashing into a tree while trying to avoid a bicyclist.

1949

- Louis Chiron, driver for the Mercedes Benz team, accuses Hellé Nice of being a Gestapo agent during the war, effectively ruining her career.

1958

- Italian Maria Teresa de Filippis becomes the first women to race in Formula One since the inauguration of the World Drivers Championship in 1950. She races in three Grand Prix events for Maserati, with a best finish of 10th at the Belgium GP.

1959

- Maria Teresa de Filippis retires from racing after failing to qualify an F2 Porsche at the Monaco GP and the tragic the death of her mentor, French racer Jean Behra.

1960

- Pat Moss-Carlsson, along with co-driver Ann Wisdom, becomes the first British woman to win the Liege–Rome–Liege rally, driving an Austin-Healey 3000.

1962

- The British Women's Racing Drivers Club is formed.

1965

- Shirley Muldowney is the first woman licensed by NHRA to drive a gasoline-burning dragster, capable of speeds over 150 miles per hour in the quarter mile.

1975

- Italian Maria Grazia "Lella" Lombardi races for the March Racing Team (12 GPs during 1975 and 1976), becoming the first woman to post a top-six placing at the Spanish GP. The race ends early due to a crash, but those who cross the finish line were awarded half points—Lombardi's sixth place earns her 0.5 points.
- Shirley Muldowney becomes the first woman to qualify in the NHRA Spring Nationals Top Fuel finals. She also becomes the first woman to break the 6.00-second barrier with a run of 5.98 seconds.

1976
- British driver Davina Gallica fails to qualify for the British GP after reintroducing the unlucky no.13 Surtees TS16 car to the circuit.

1977
- Janet Guthrie becomes the first woman to qualify for the Indy 500 at a speed of 188.403 miles per hour and eventually finishes the race in 29th place.
- Shirley Muldowney becomes the first Top Fuel driver to win three back-to-back NHRA national events.

1978
- Janet Guthrie finishes ninth at the Indy 500.

1980
- South African Desire Wilson fails to qualify for the British GP but wins the Aurora AFX round at UK's Brands Hatch circuit.

1981
- French driver Michele Mouton becomes the first woman to win a round of the Rally World Championship, scoring a victory at the San Remo Rally.
- Shirley Muldowney wins the 1981 AHRA World Championship —the first and only woman to do so.

1982
- Diane Teel, a school bus driver from Virginia, becomes the first female driver to qualify for the Busch series of NASCAR. She starts in and finishes in 10th place at Martinsville.
- Michele Mouton and her co-driver Fabrizia Pons win the rallies of Portugal, Brazil and Acropolis, and finish second overall in the Rally World Championship.
- Shirley Muldowney wins the Winston World Championship, the first person in history to claim the title three times.

1983
- British rally driver Louise Aitken-Walker becomes the first woman to win a national championship round outright in Britain, and she also wins the Coupes des Dames at the Monte Carlo Rally.

1984
- Lyn St. James is awarded the IMSA Camel GT Rookie of the Year.

1985
- Lyn St. James is named IMSA Norelco Driver of the Year.
- Michele Mouton becomes the first women to win the Race of Pike's Peak.

1986

- Bunny Burkett becomes the first-ever IHRA female Funny Car World Champion.

1987

- Louise Aitken-Walker is voted National Driver of the Year by readers of British magazine *Autosport*.

1990

- Louise Aitken-Walker wins the Ladies World Rally Championship.
- Lyn St. James becomes President of the Women's Sports Foundation, which provides opportunities and support for female athletes in many sports.

1991

- Louise Aitken-Walker wins both the Jim Clark Trophy and the Seagrove Trophy.

1992

- Giovanna Amati signs with the Brabham team to race F1, but leaves after failing to qualify for the first three races of the season.
- Lyn St. James is the first woman to be awarded Indy 500 Rookie of the Year.

1993

- The Lyn St. James Foundation is established to raise awareness of automotive safety and driver development, especially for budding female race drivers.

1994

- Shawna Robinson becomes the first woman to win the pole position in a major NASCAR race at the Busch series in Atlanta, Georgia.

1995

- Sarah Fisher is named the Dirt Track Racing Round-Up Rookie of the Year.

1996

- Amanda Whitaker becomes the first female to win a British National Single Seater Championship winning the Monoposto Championship.
- Shirley Muldowney sets a new IHRA speed record at 294.98 miles per hour.

1997

- Sarah Fisher is named to the 62-race All-Star Circuit of Champions series, where she scores a hard-fought second-place finish at Eldora Speedway.

1999

- Louise Smith becomes the first woman inducted into the International Motorsports Hall of Fame in Talladega, Alabama.
- Sarah Fisher becomes the youngest person ever to pass the Indy Racing League Rookie Test.

And into the new millennium....

2001

- Barbara Armstrong scores an impressive second-overall finish in the World Cup Rally in her favorite Peugeot.
- Shirley Muldowney runs a career best of 4.64 seconds elapsed time at 320.20 miles per hour.
- Danica Patrick is awarded the Gorsline Scholarship Award for Top Upcoming Road Racing Driver.
- Ashley Taws is recruited by Mattel and Wal-Mart to drive the pink and purple "Be Anything with Barbie at Wal-Mart" Ford race car.
- Jutta Kleinschmidt, a former motorbike champion, wins the Paris–Dakar rally, considered by many to be the toughest rally in the world, and becomes the first woman to ever do so.

2002

- Erin Crocker is awarded the Outstanding Newcomer Award from the National Sprint Car Hall of Fame and is subsequently bombarded with national media attention.
- Katherine Legge becomes the first woman to be honored as one of the British Racing Drivers' Club Rising Stars.

2004

- Laleh Seddigh is finally granted permission to compete against male drivers by the national auto racing federation of Iran.
- Shirley Muldowney is inducted into the International Motor Sports Hall of Fame.

2005

- Janet Guthrie's autobiography, entitled *Janet Guthrie: A Life at Full Throttle*, is published.
- Danica Patrick finishes in fourth place at the Indy 500, setting a new women's record for highest finish.
- Erin Crocker becomes the first woman ever to participate in the Evernham development program and launches her NASCAR Busch and Craftsman Truck series career.

- Melanie Troxel clocks a 4.458 second pass and a top speed of 330.31 miles per hour at the Dallas drag strip and becomes the track's all-time quickest female driver.

2006

- Belgian Vanina Ickx, daughter of legendary racer Jacky Ickx, is appointed the new Audi works driver and becomes the first woman in the DTM since 1995. Vanina starts her career at the age of 21 in 1996, and after success in touring cars, she wins a podium position at the 24-Hours of Spa–Francorchamps and then competes in the grueling Dakar Rally.
- Bunny Burkett returns to racing for a final appearance at the Maryland International Raceway for the Ford Fever Classic at the age of 61. She drives her 2006 Dodge Avenger Top Alcohol Funny Car to a 5.99 elapsed time on the scoreboards at over 240 miles per hour.
- Janet Guthrie is inducted into the International Motorsports Hall of Fame.
- Laleh Seddigh is awarded her International Racing Driving License during the BMW School Series at the Bahrain International Circuit in Manama.
- Leilani Münter becomes the first woman to qualify in the 45-year history of the Bettenhausen Classic at Illiana Speedway, Indiana.

2007

- Ashley Force becomes only the 10th woman ever licensed to drive a Funny Car.
- Simona de Silvestro becomes the first woman to ever earn a podium finish at the Indianapolis Motor Speedway, with a pair of third-place FBMWUSA results at the 2006 U.S. Grand Prix.

And whatever the future may hold…

While European racing circuits accepted female drivers as serious contenders many years ago, glamour has finally taken over the North American tracks with the likes of Danica Patrick, Leilani Munter and hot-rodding media darlings Ashley, Brittany and Courtney Force, all of who bring more than just glitz and sex appeal to the tracks; there can be no disputing the skill and winning performances that these ladies deliver.

Notes on Sources

www.insideracingnews.com

www.girlracer.co.uk

www.racerchicks.com

www.motor-sport.uk.com

www.historicracing.com

www.brooklands.org

www.speed-queens.com

BUGATTI QUEEN: In Search of a French Racing Legend (Random House)

The National Hot Rod Association (US)

www.dragracecentral.com

www.bunnyburkett.com

NASCAR.com

Int'l Motorsports Hall of Fame

Inside Racing News

USA Today

CNN

Lifetime Network

Car & Driver magazine

Telegraph Newspaper (UK)

BBC UK News

Motorsport News

The Globe & Mail Newspaper

Sports Illustrated

Inside Track

Sports Image Times

Sporting News Publishing Co.

Inside Track magazine

Kalitta Racing

NHRA

Eurosport News

USA Today

New York Times

BBC Sports

ESPN

Fox Sports

TSN

Drag Race USA

www.indycar.com

Glenda Fordham

Glenda Fordham has led an exciting, albeit stationary life working in the entertainment field for over 30 years, promoting and managing music and variety performers, as well as teaching business management to film and music students.

Her love of auto racing started in the 60s when she was still a youngster growing up in the Australian bush, watching Stirling Moss and Jackie Stewart race around tracks in exotic locales on her family's black and white TV console. She often wondered why there were no female drivers, no role models for her own dreams of speed and freedom which probably accounts for the fact that she still does not have a driver's license!

Doing research for this book, Glenda has proven once and for all that women did indeed compete back in the early days of auto racing, but were never given their due in the history books. During the writing of this book, Glenda was privileged to get to know several of today's top women racers who risk everything to pursue their dreams.

A regular contributor to Canada's national newspapers and magazines, Glenda has written three previous books on Formula One and stock car racing, *Formula 1 Drivers, Hottest Stock Car Drivers* and *Greatest Stock Car Races*, all published by OverTime Books.